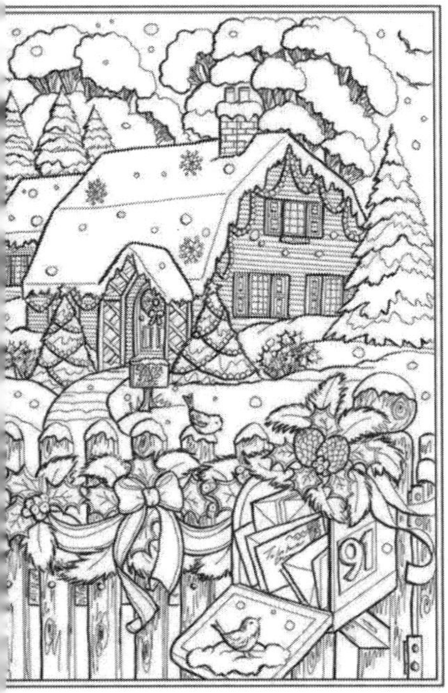

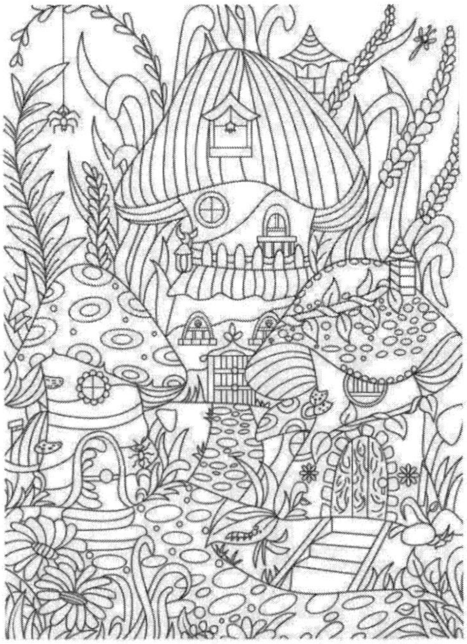

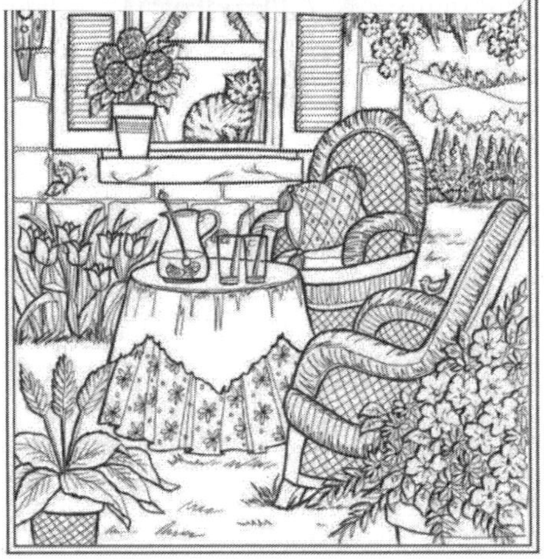

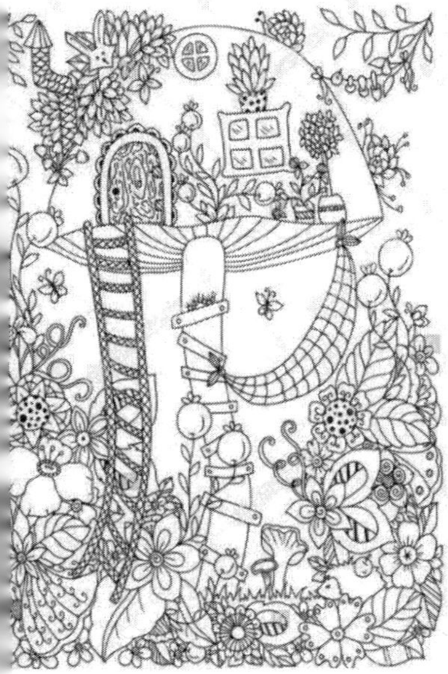

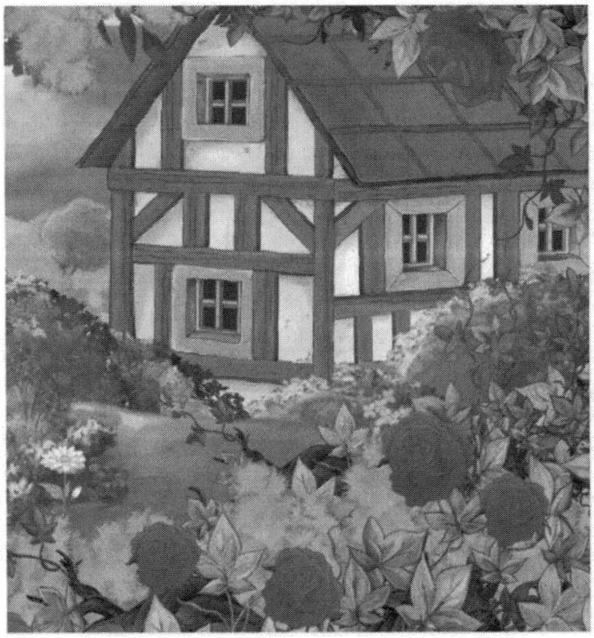

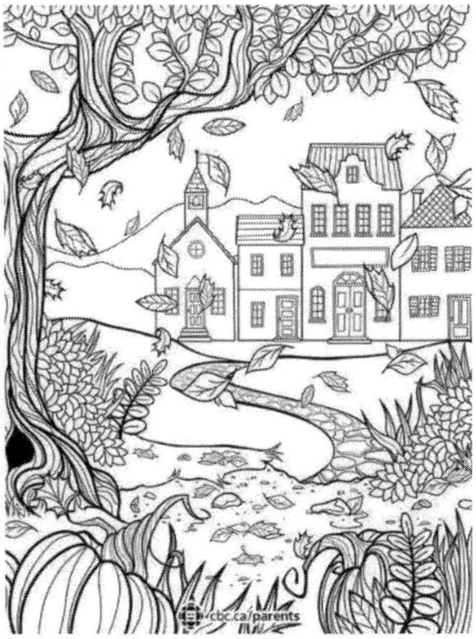
cbc.ca/parents

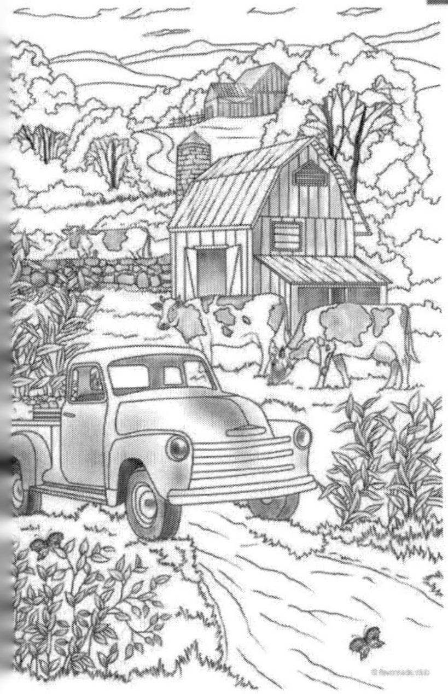

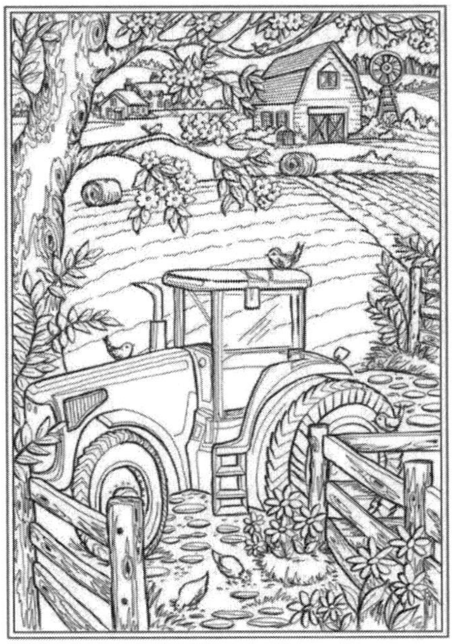

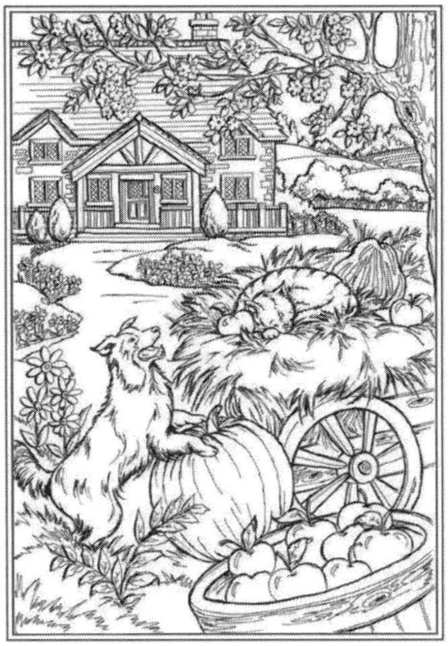

This Book Belongs To

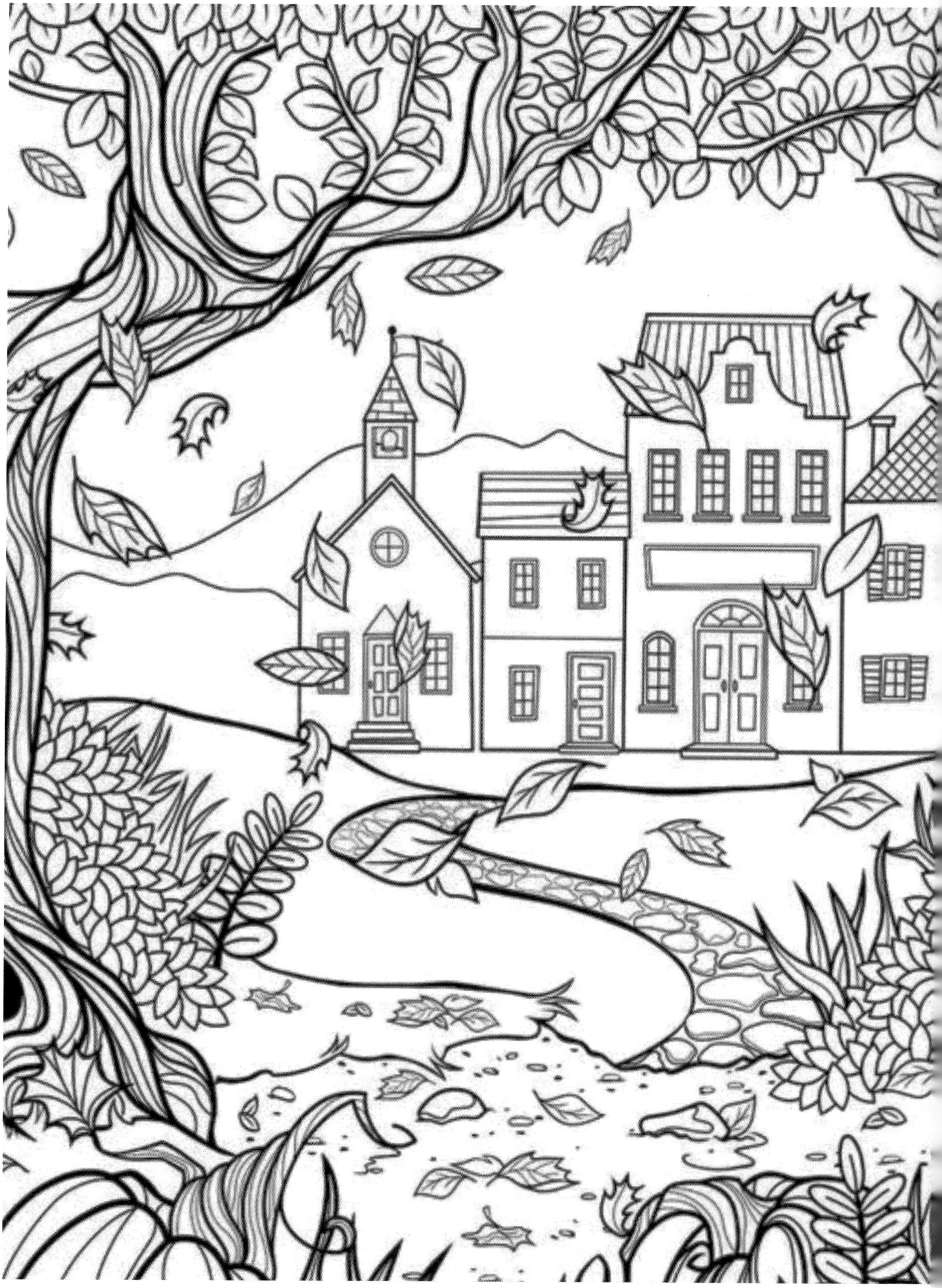

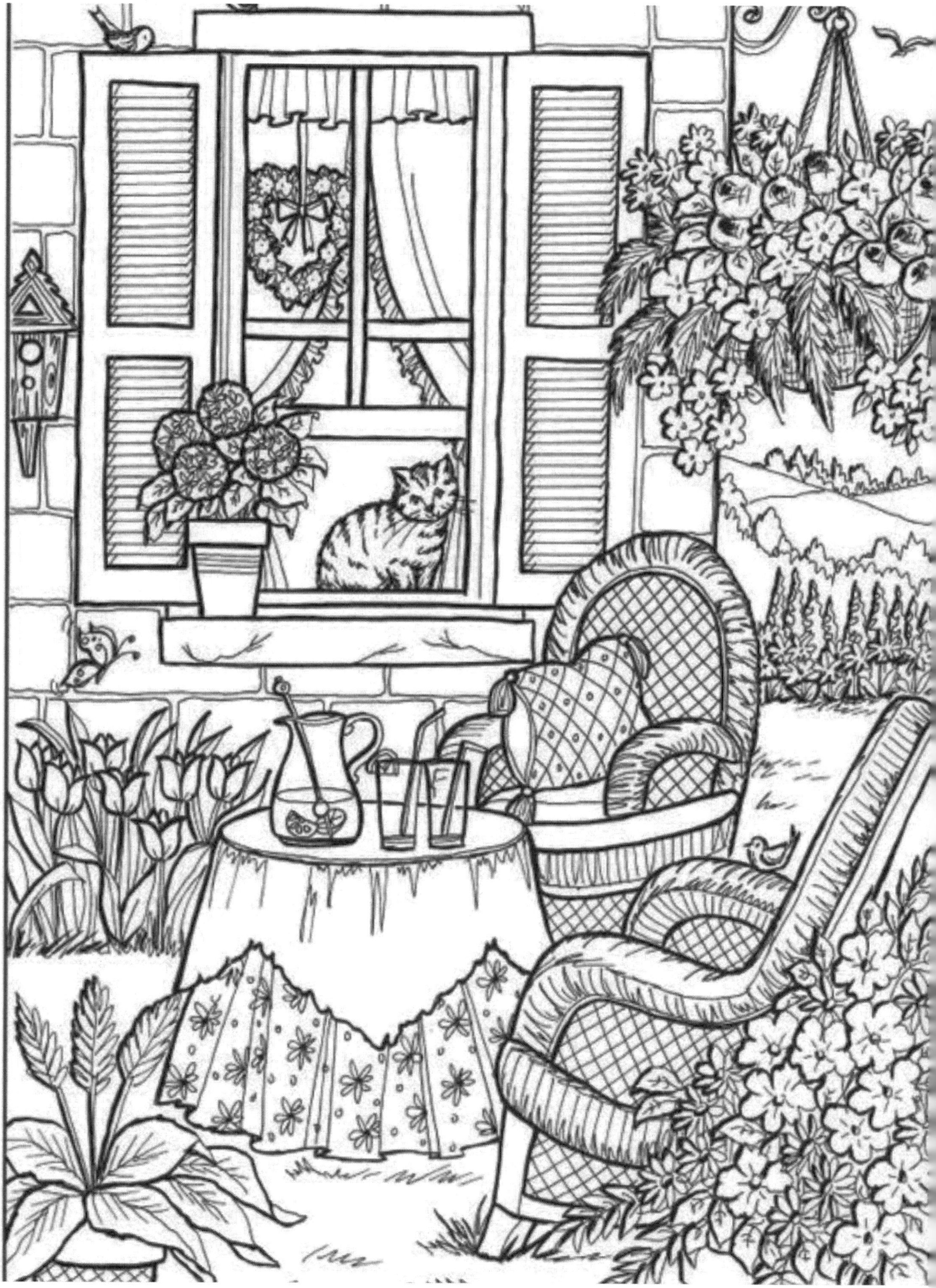

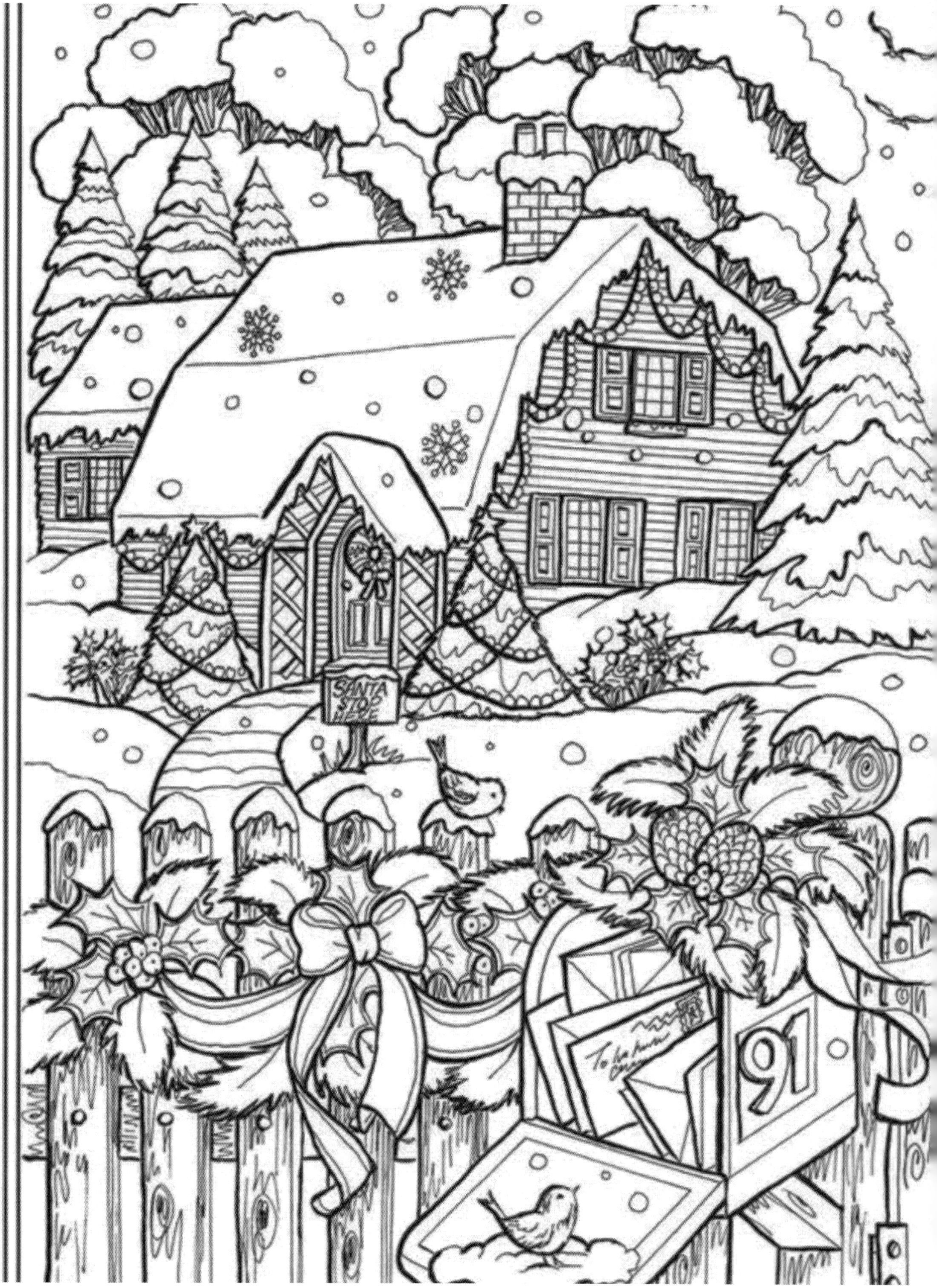
SANTA STOP HERE
91

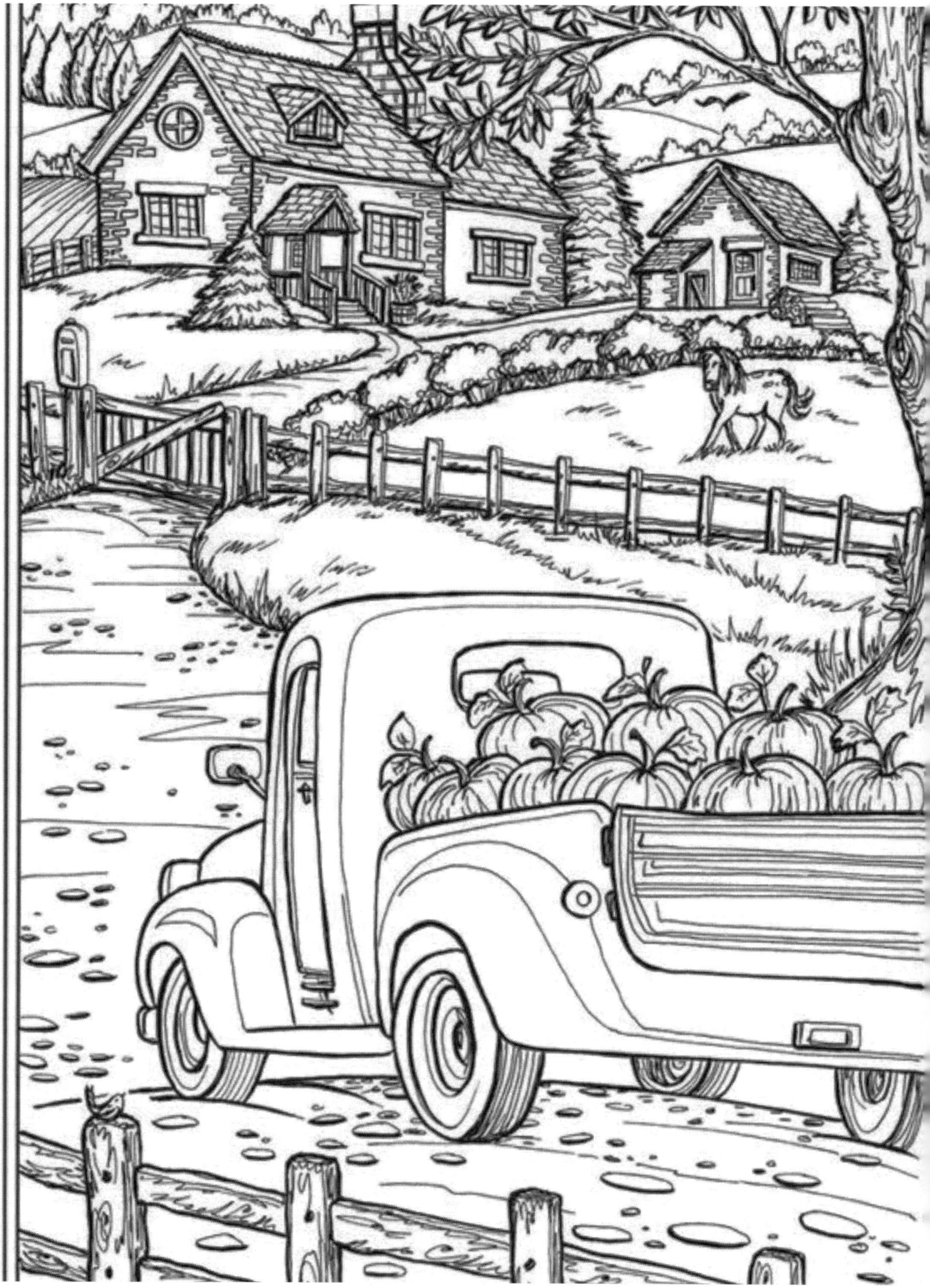

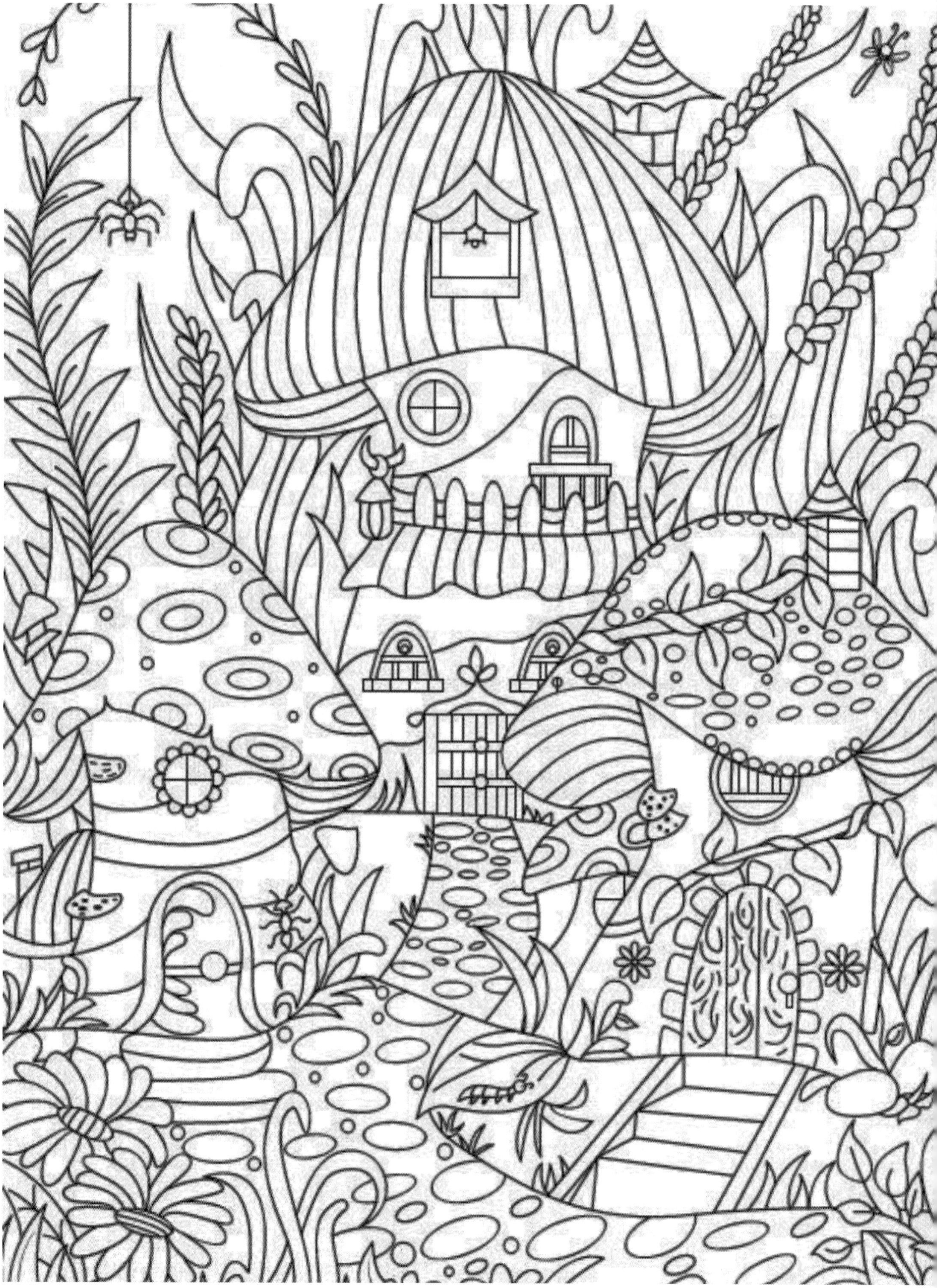

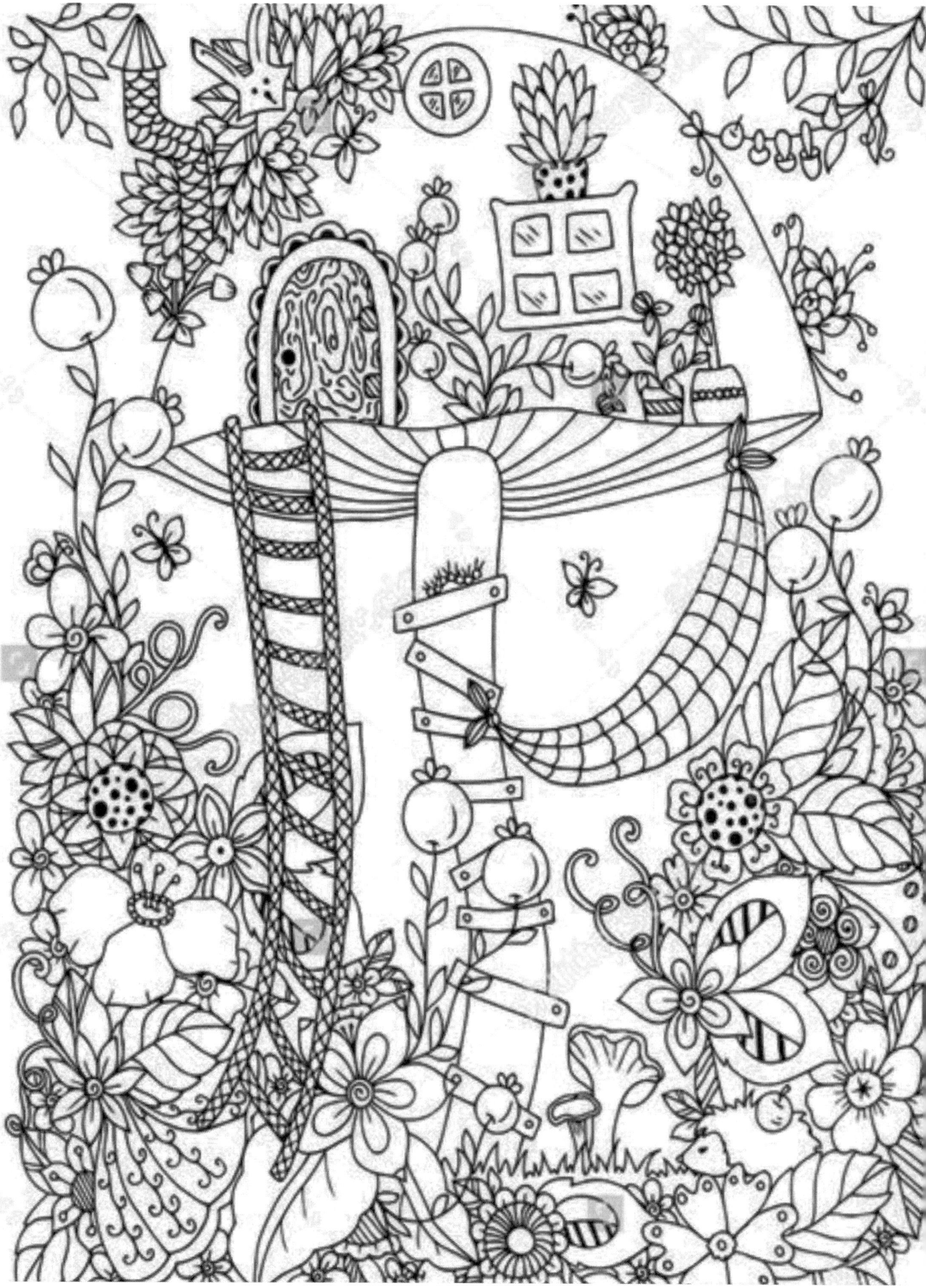

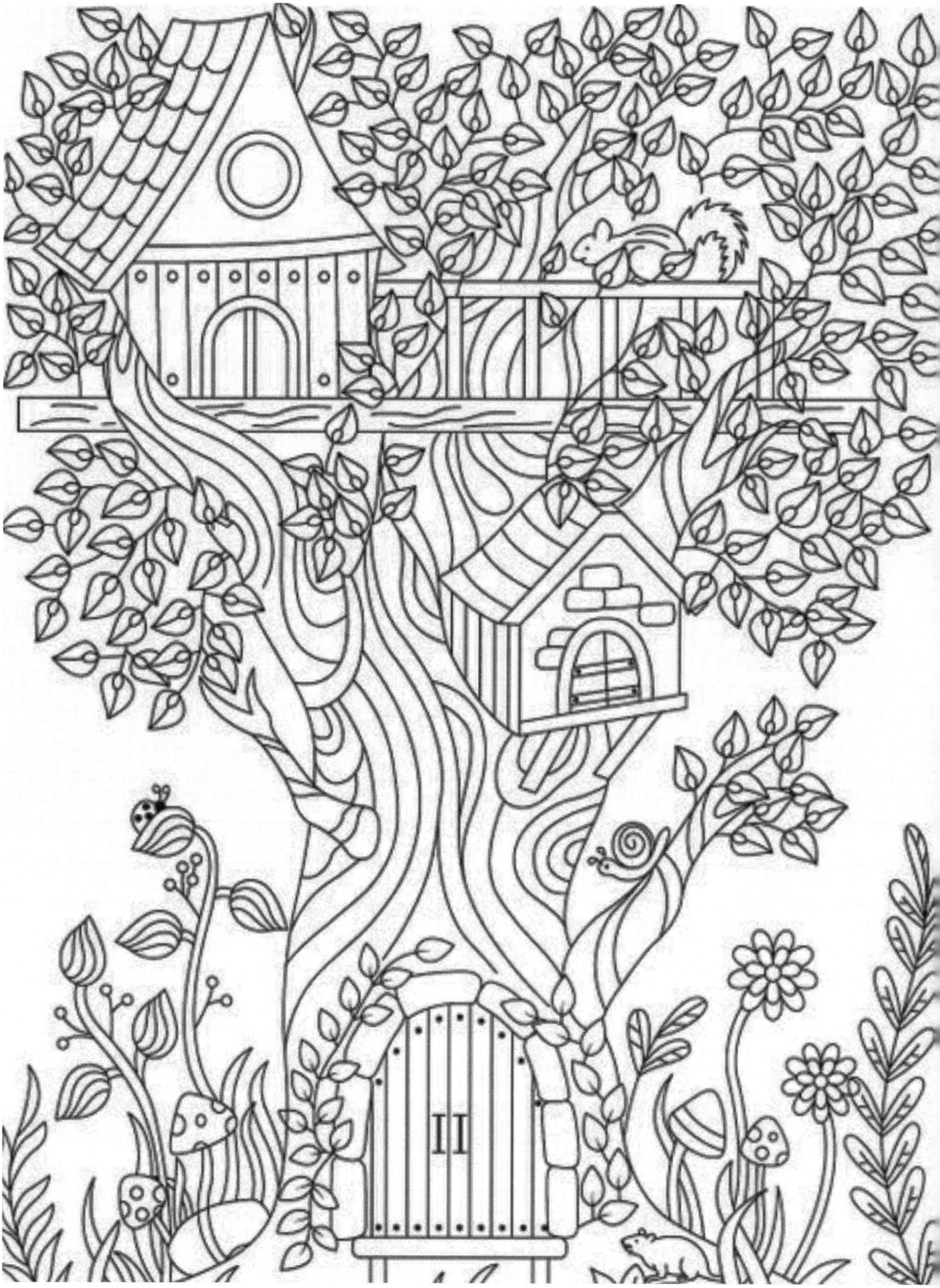

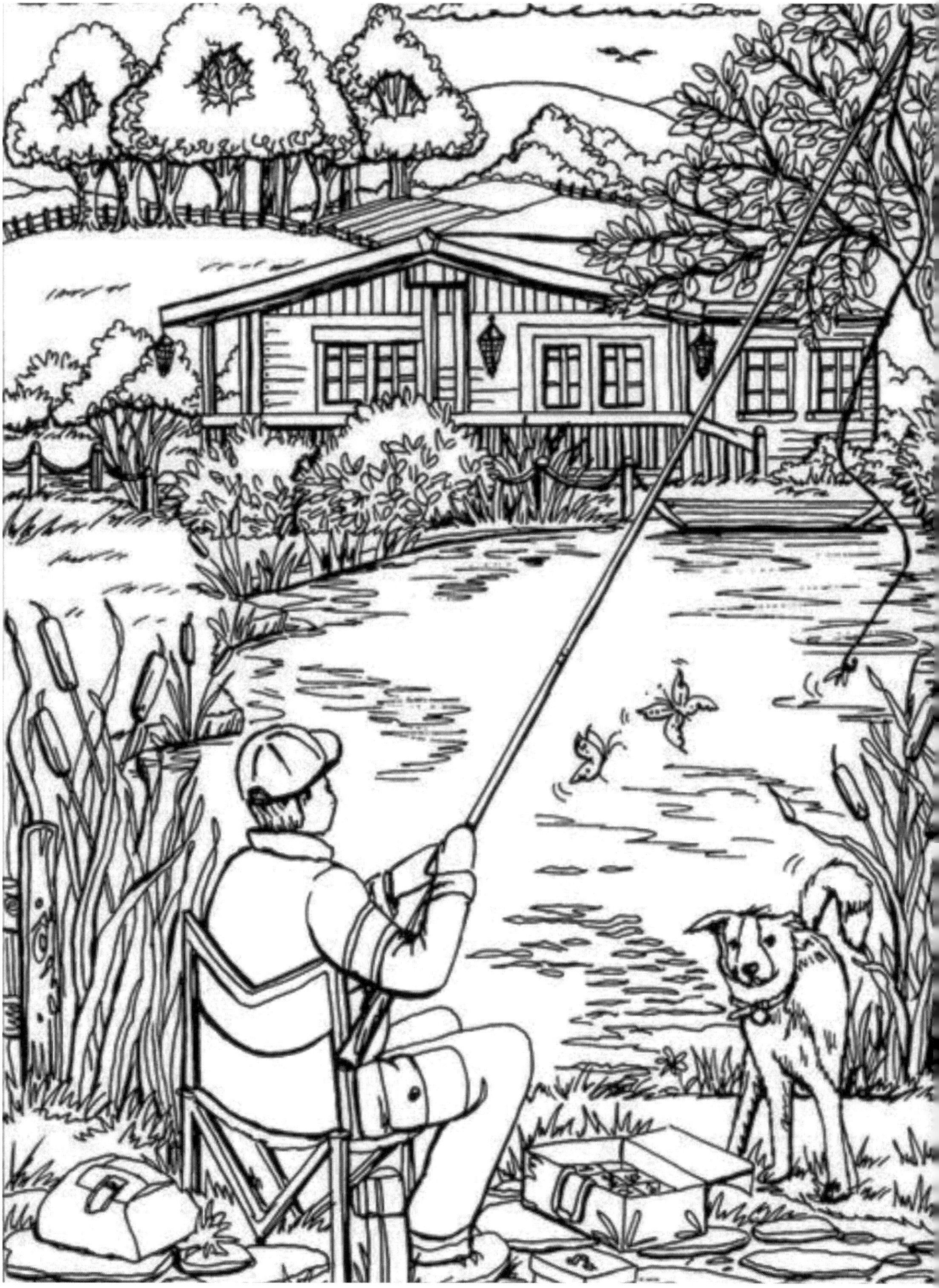

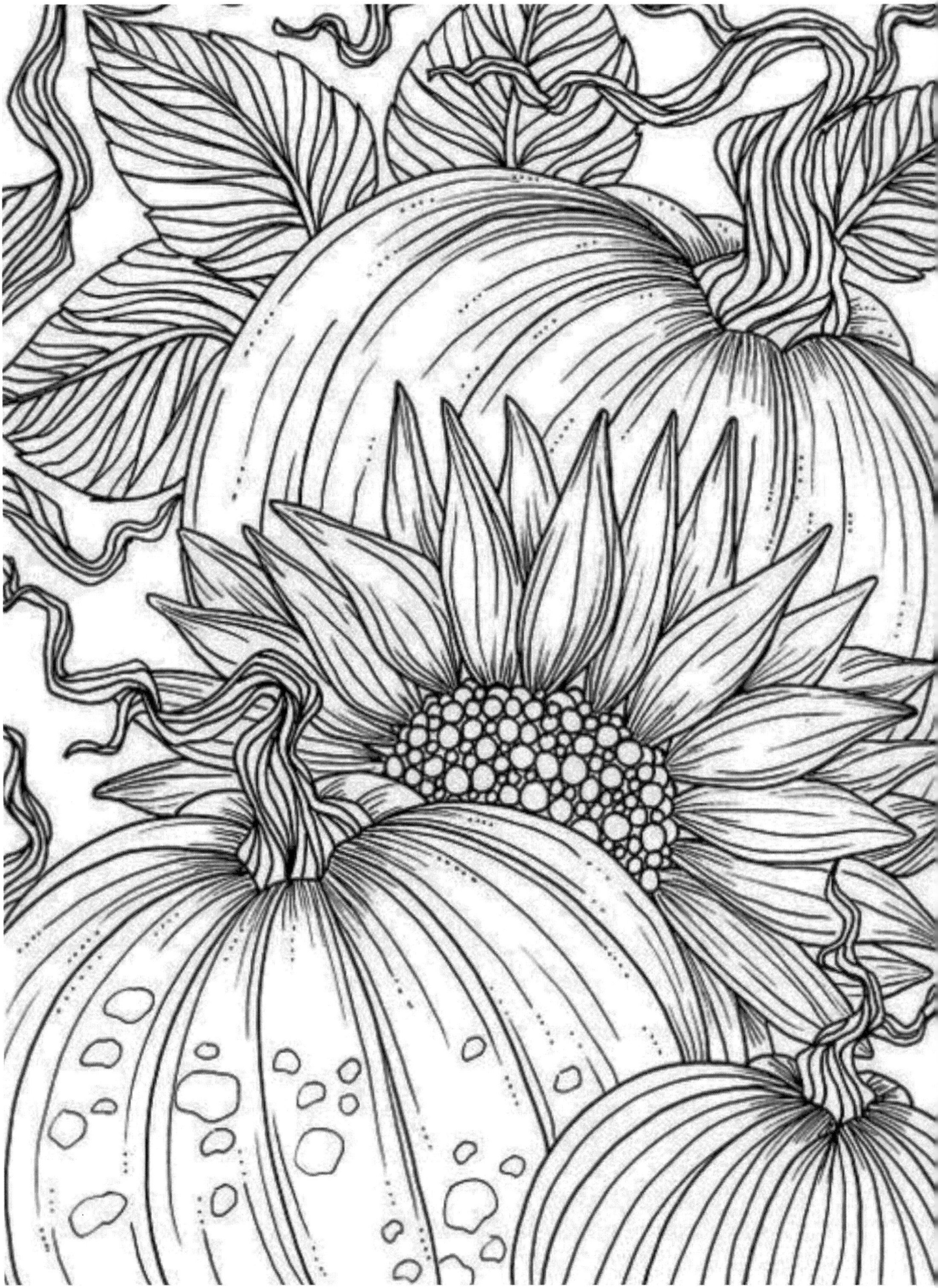

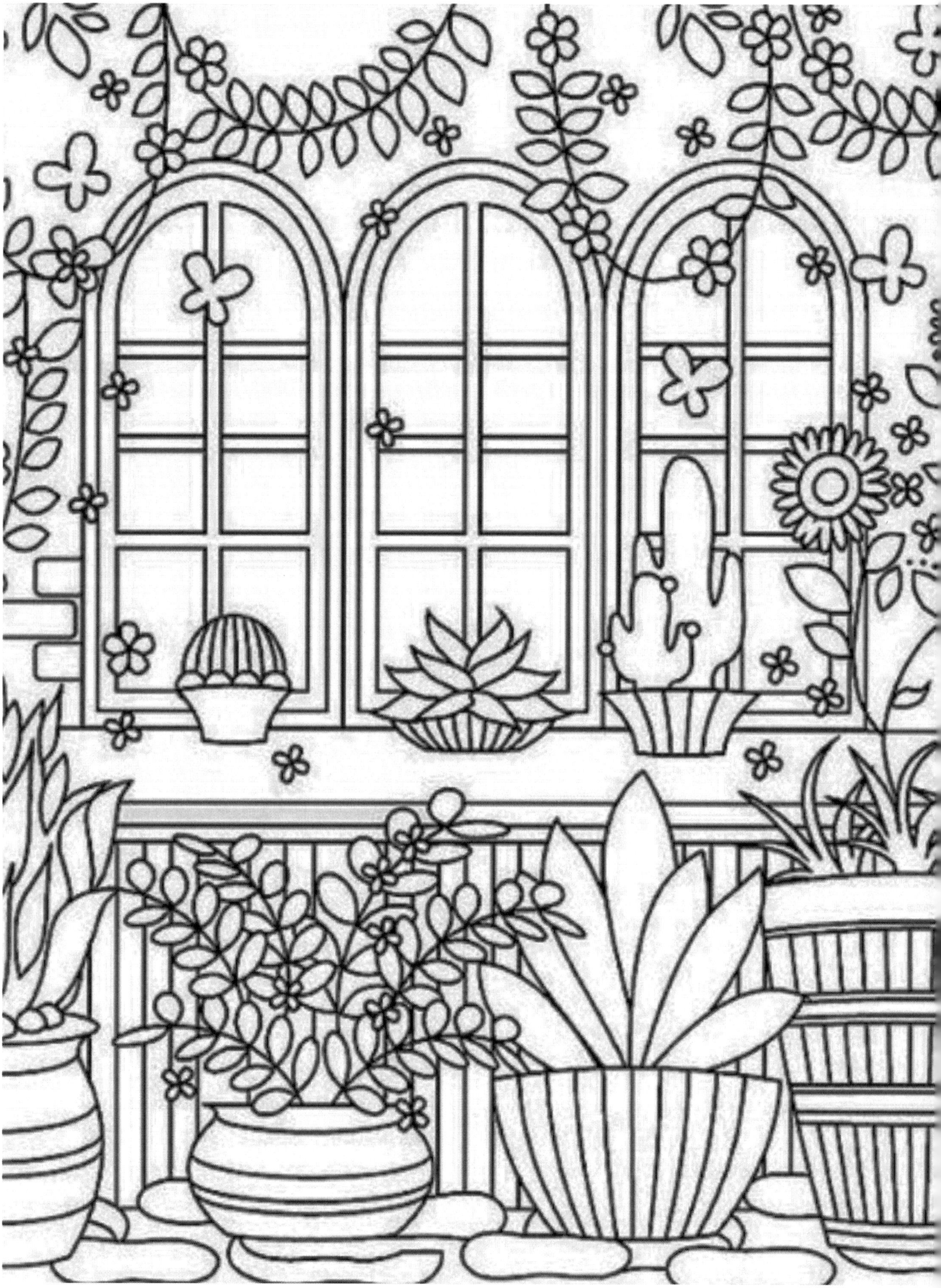

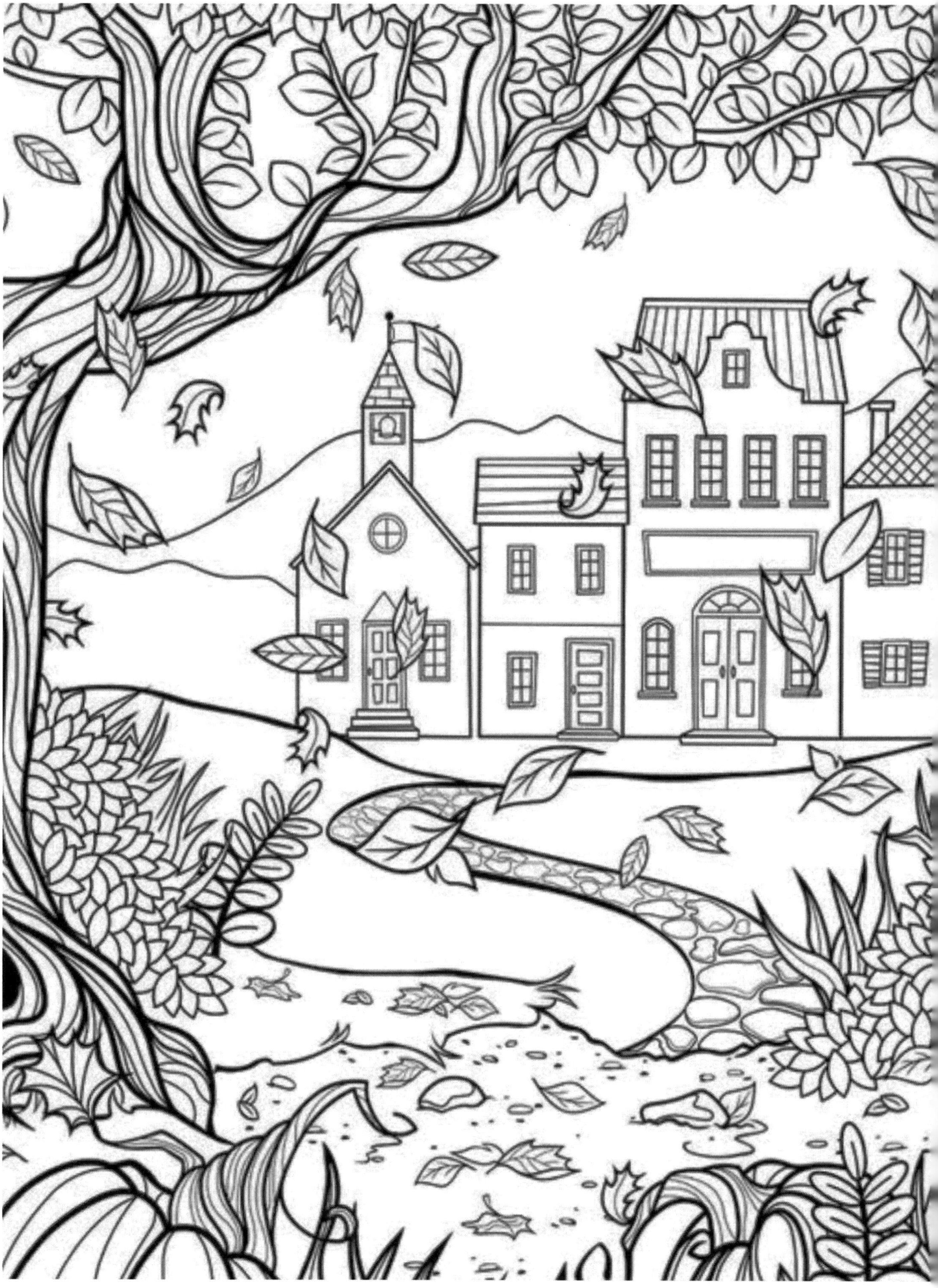

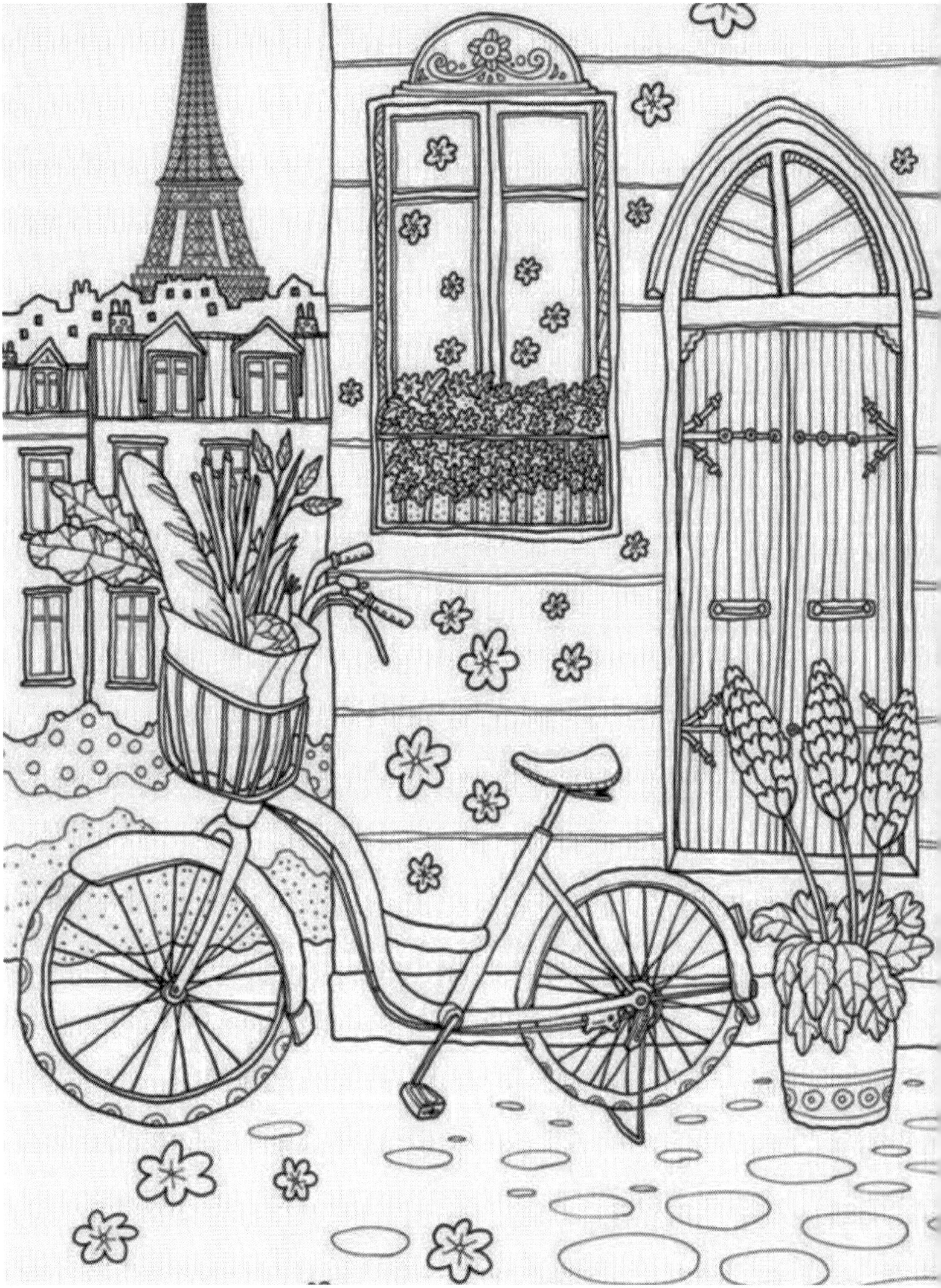

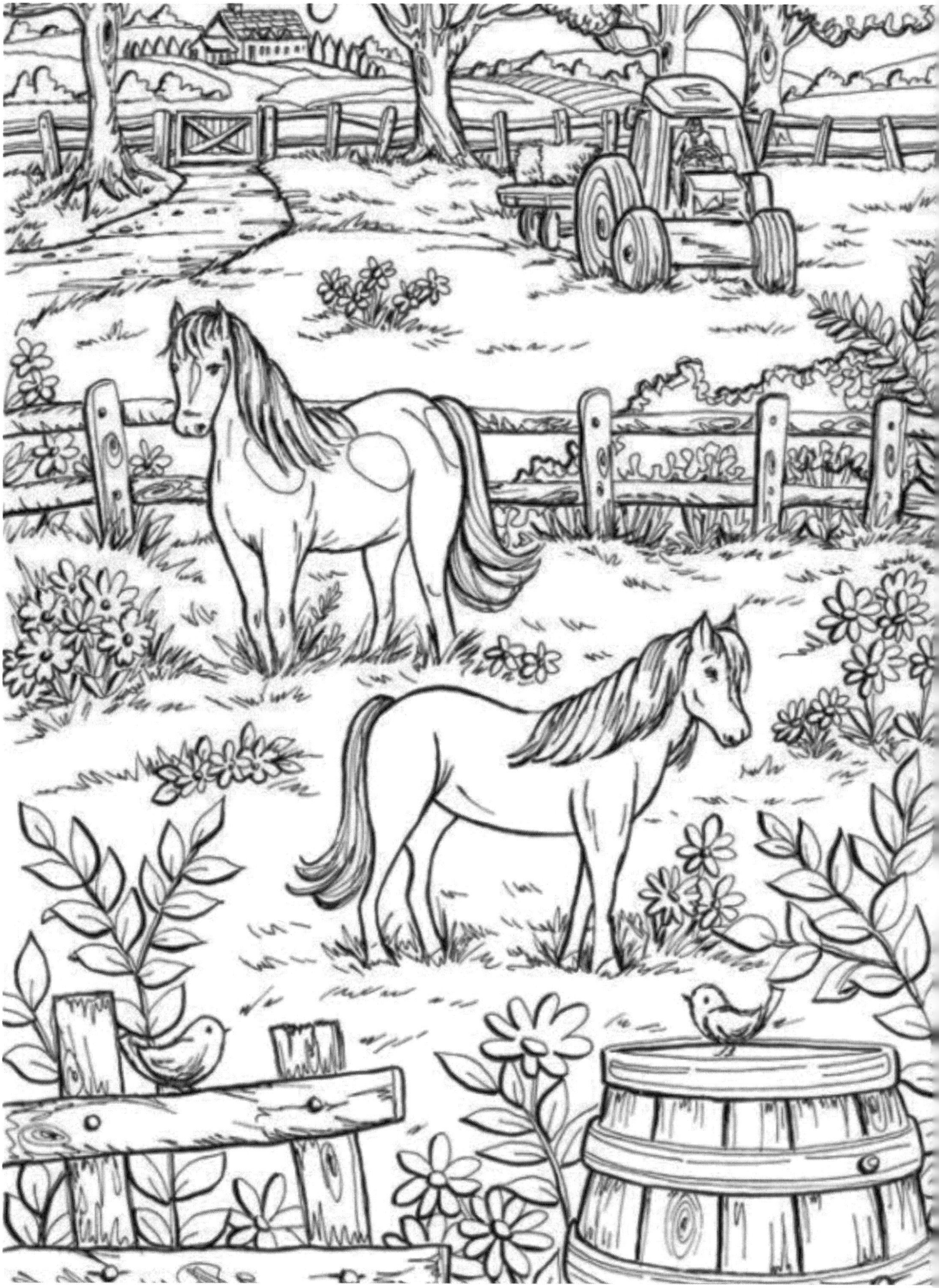

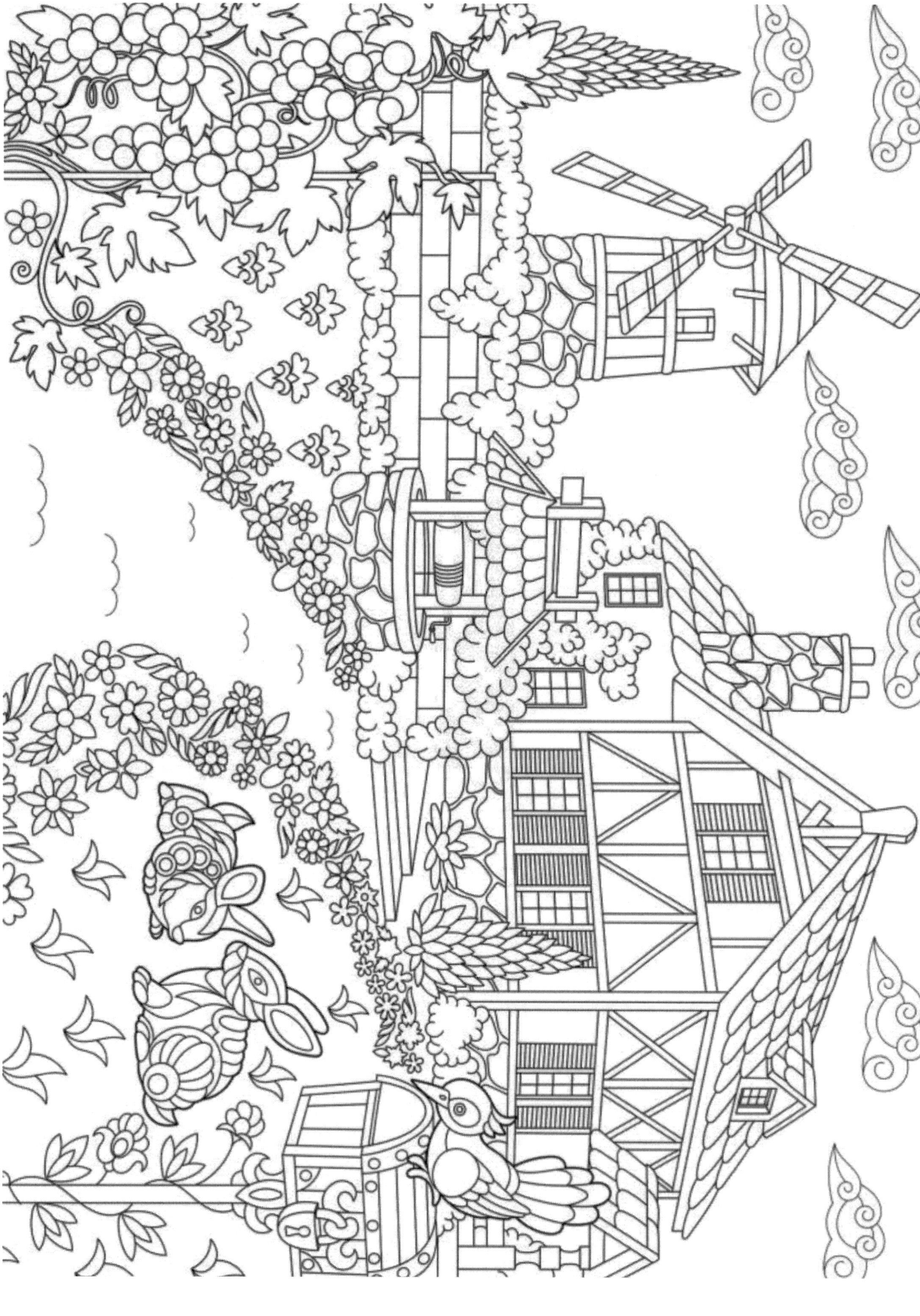

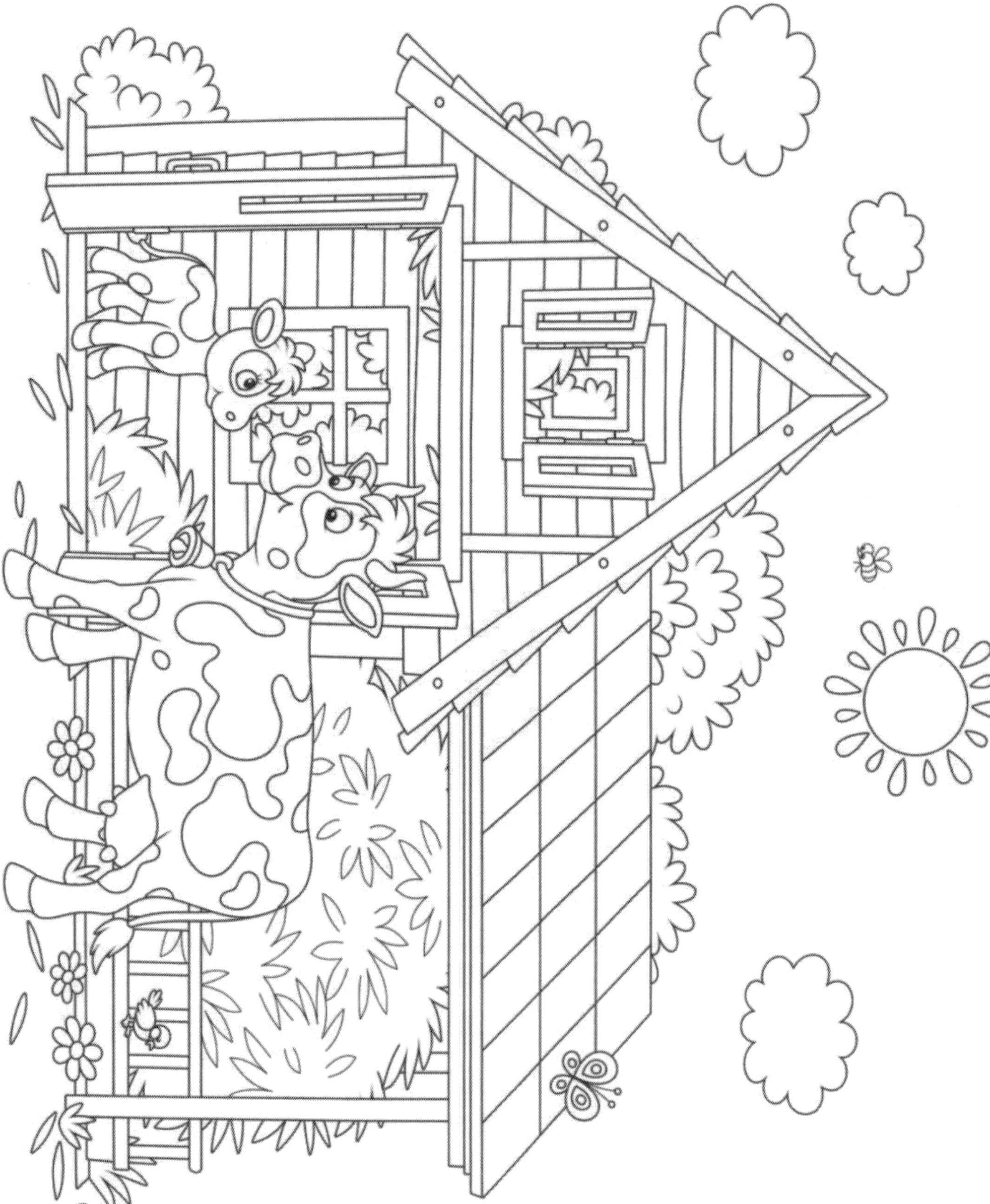

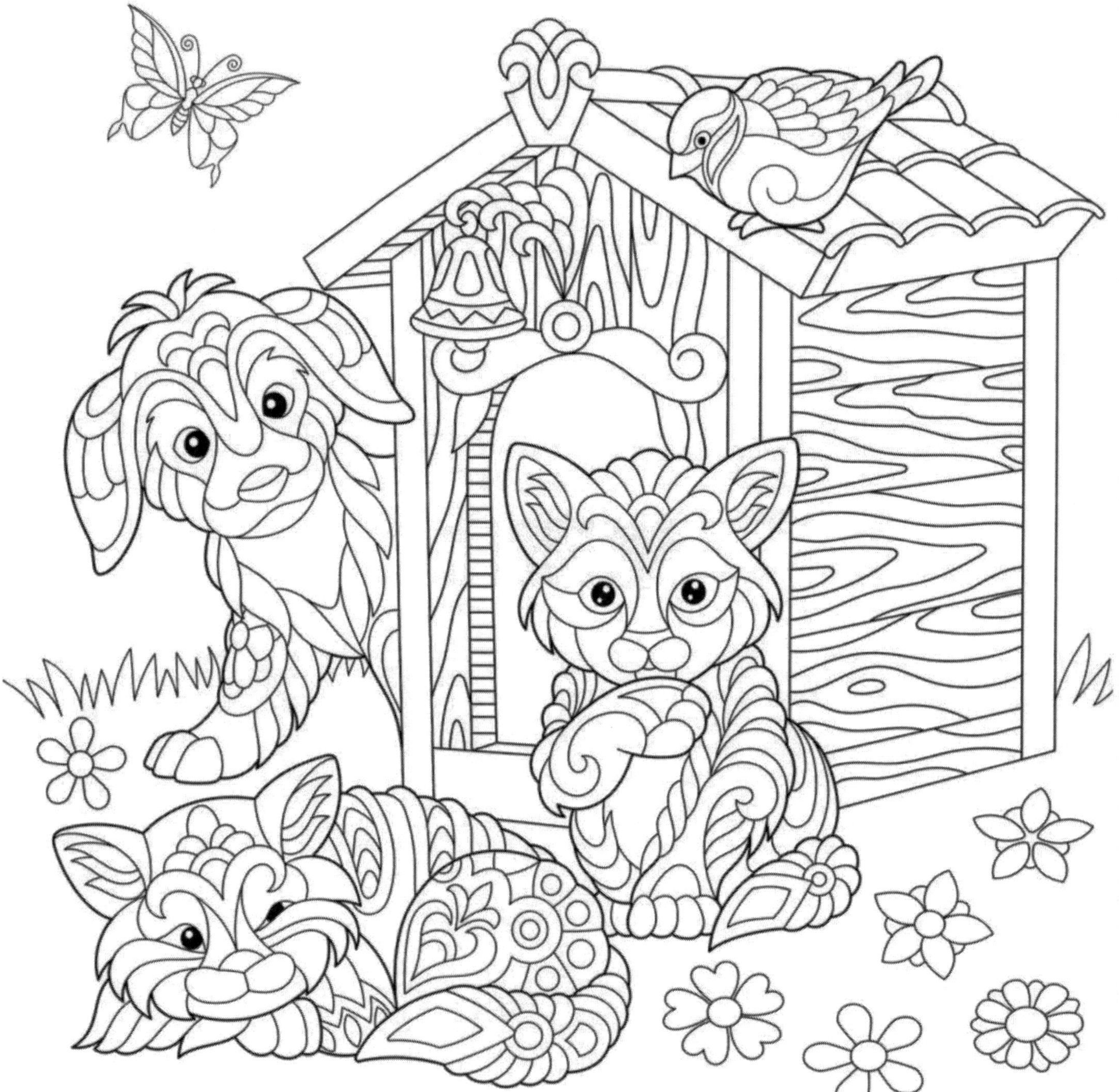

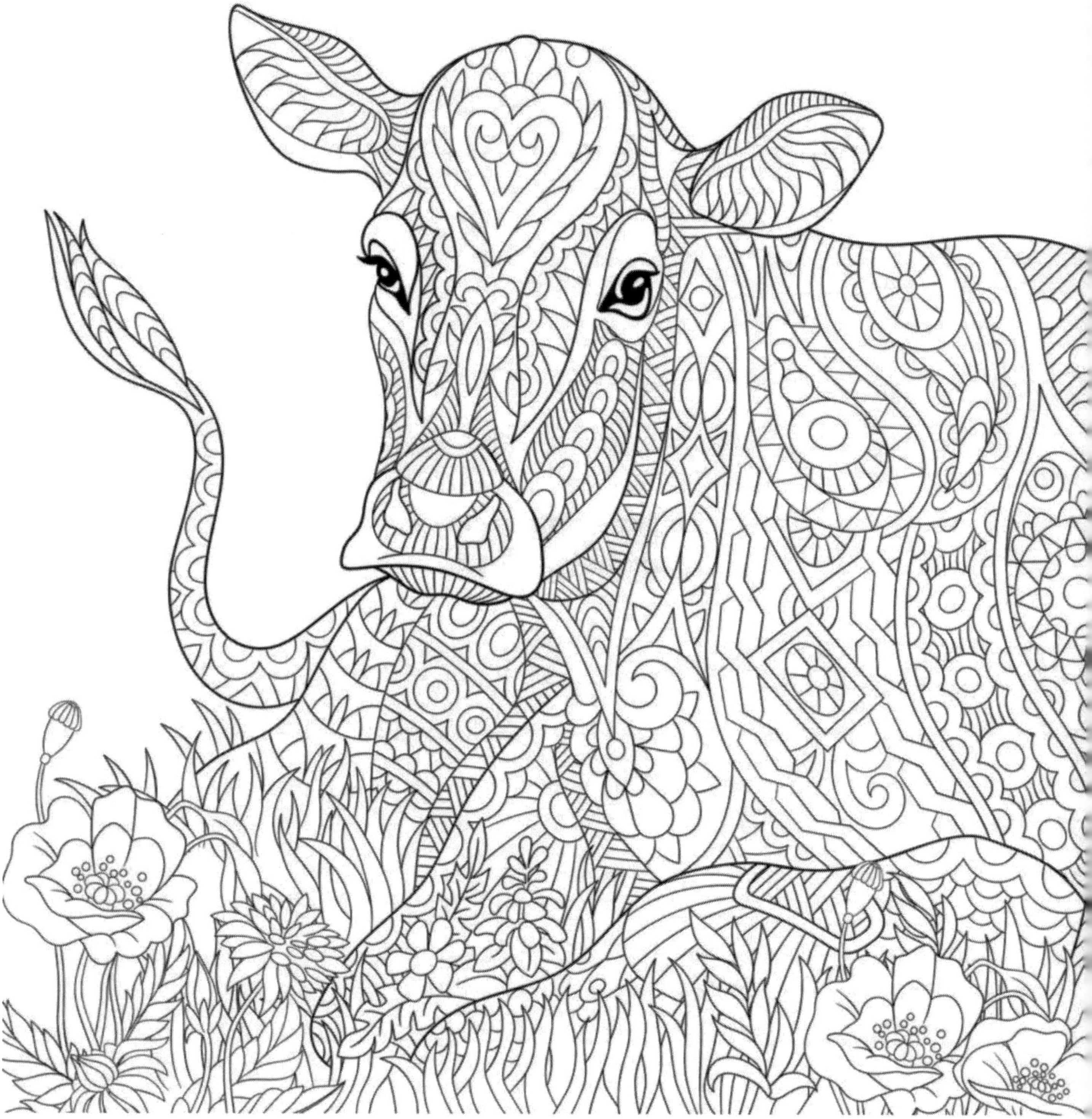

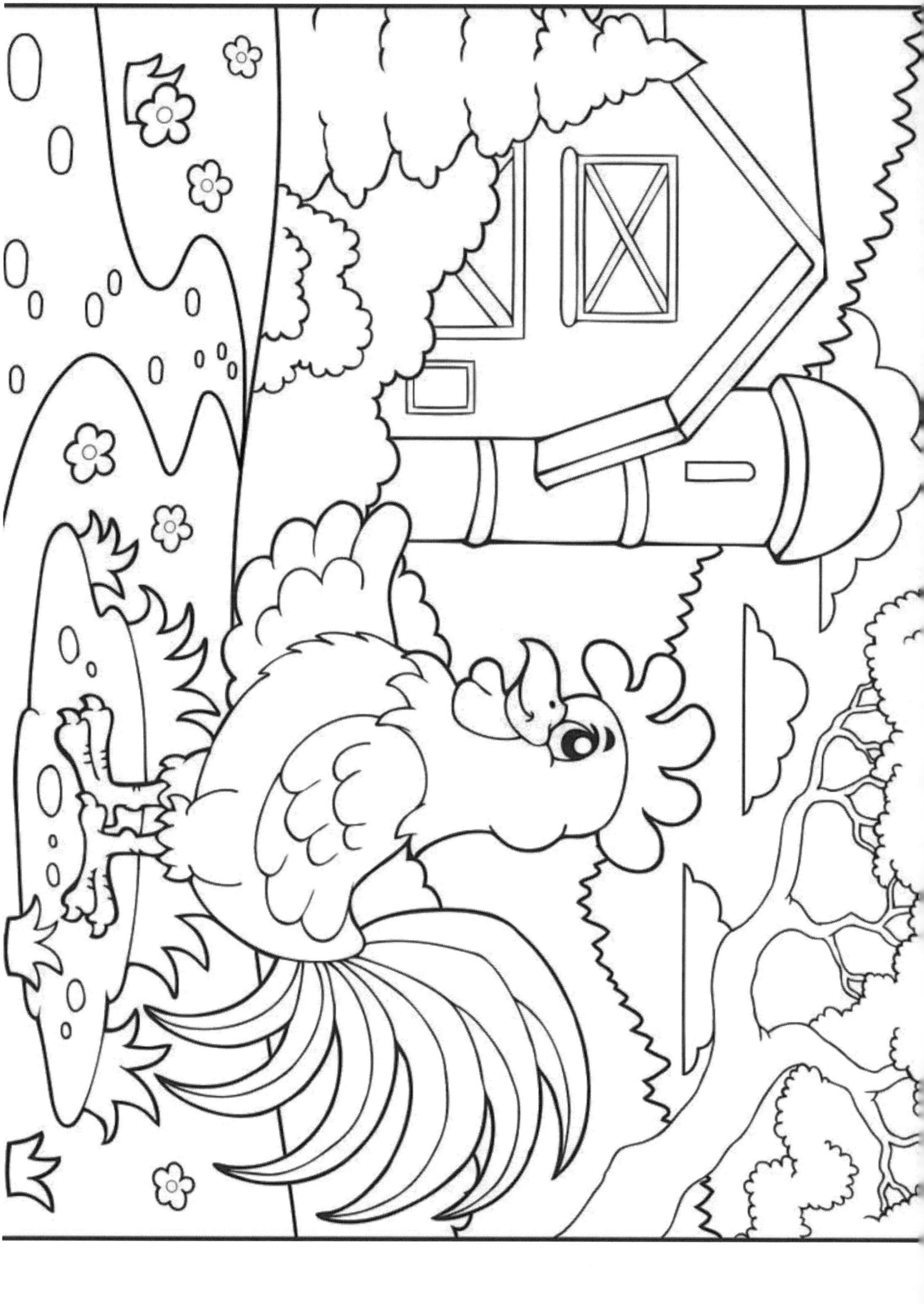

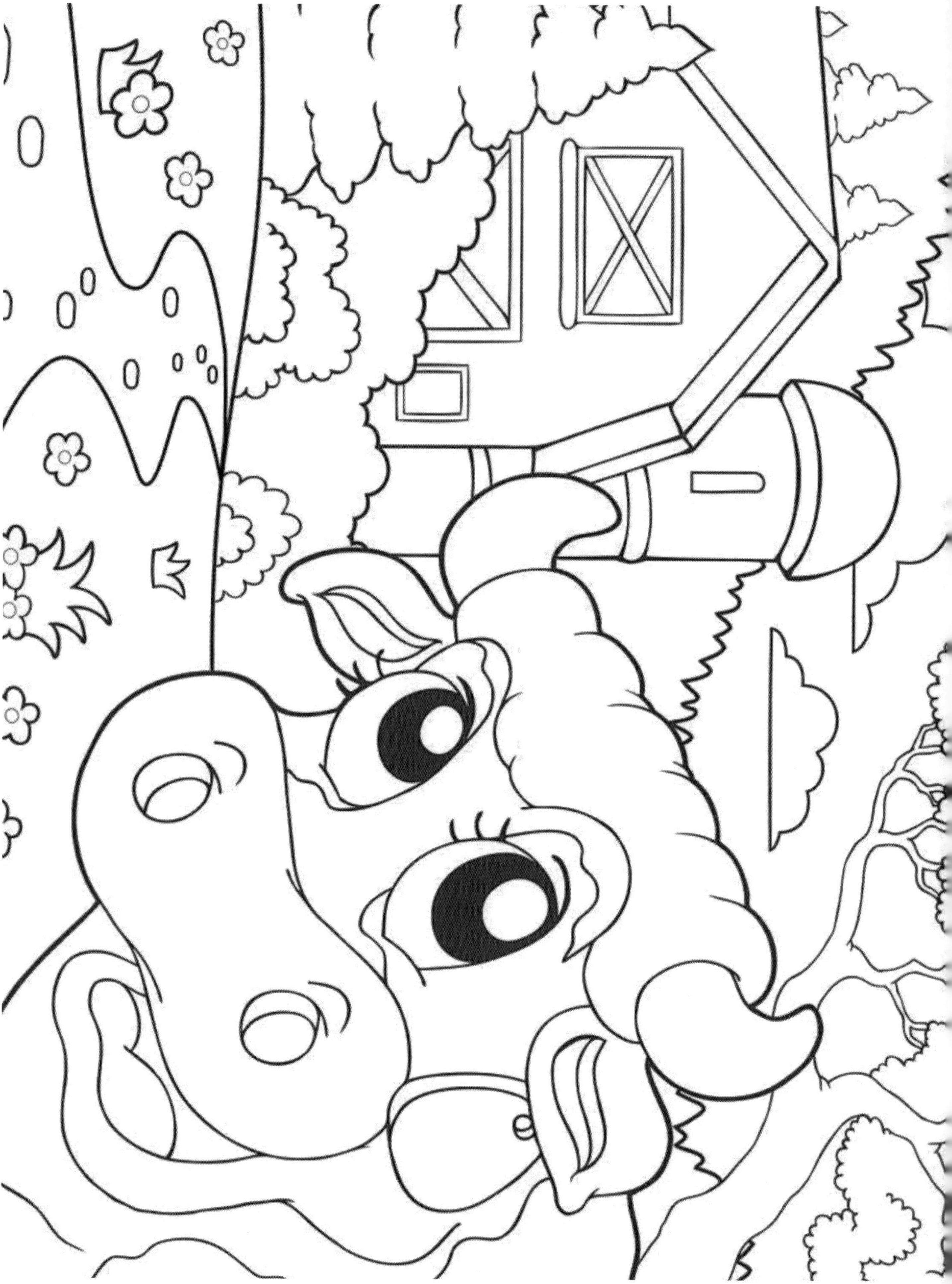

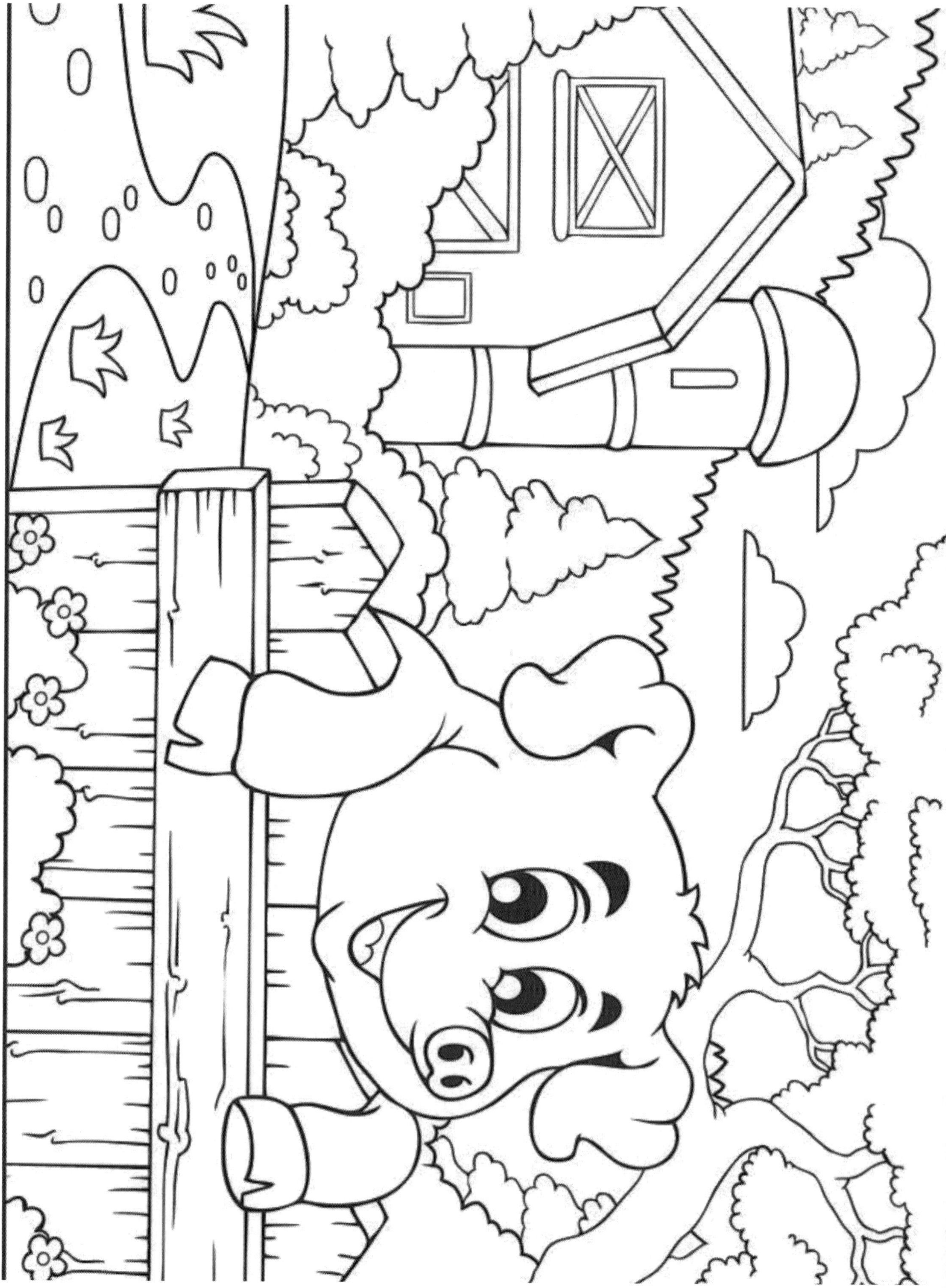

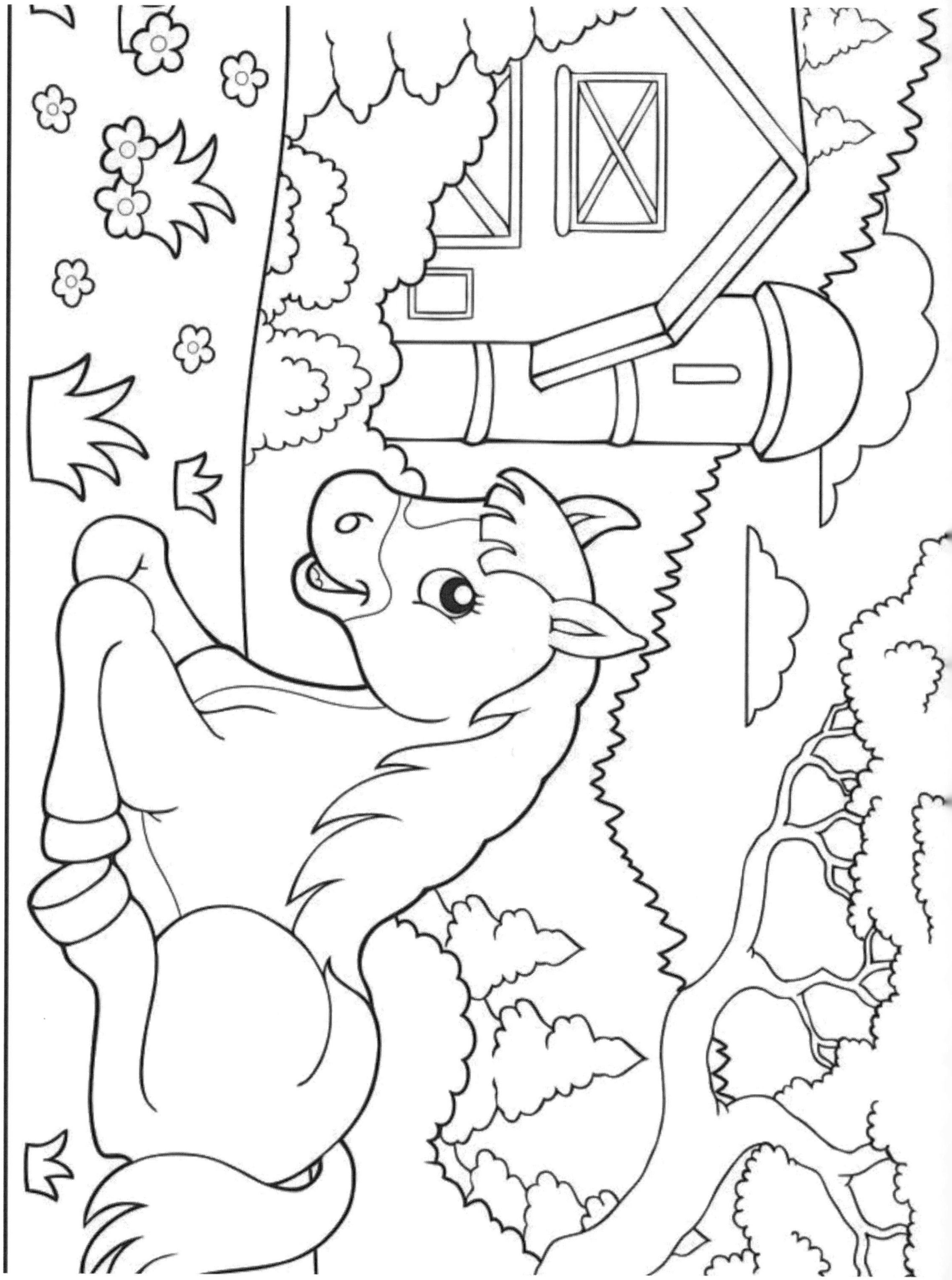

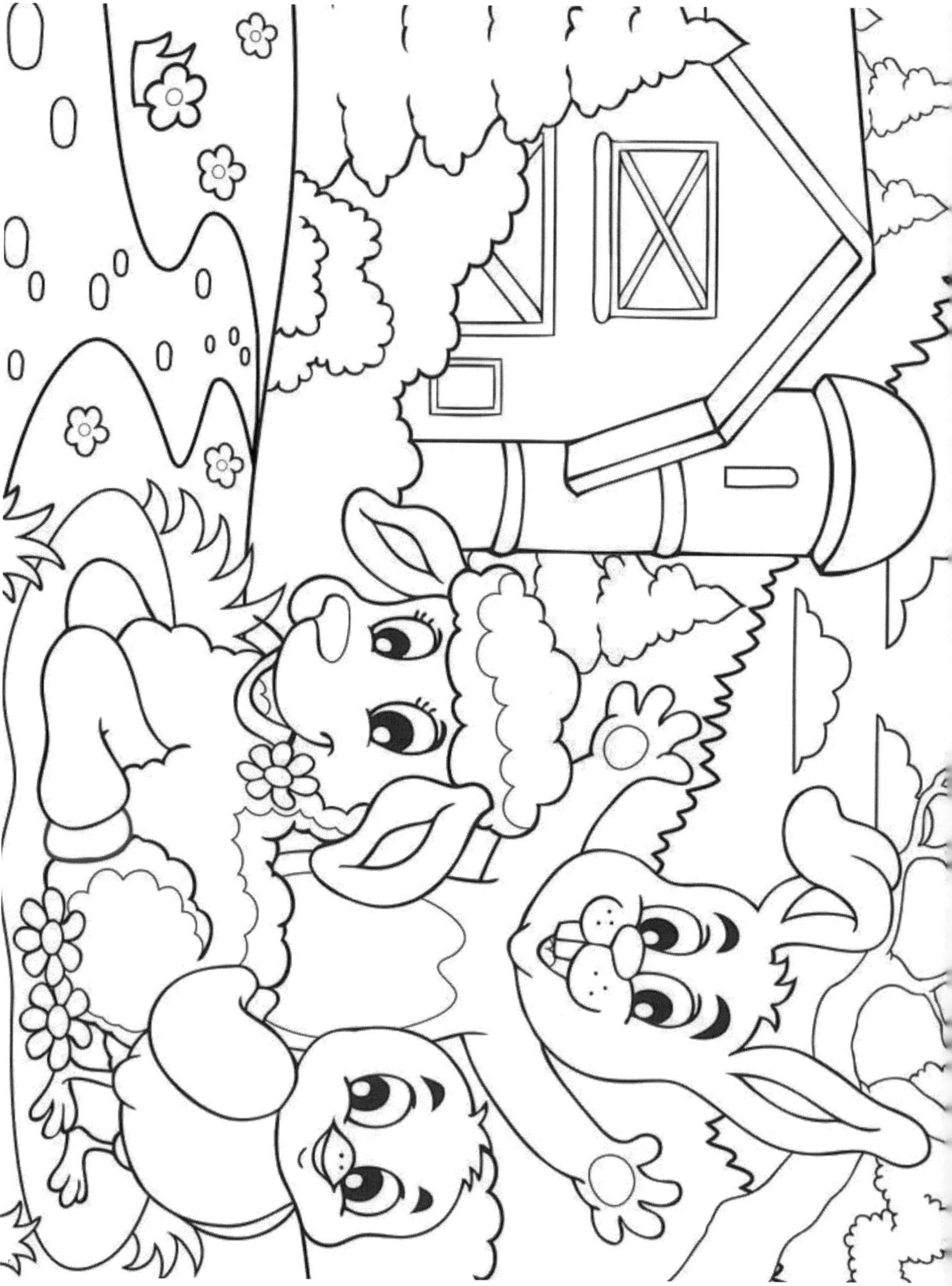

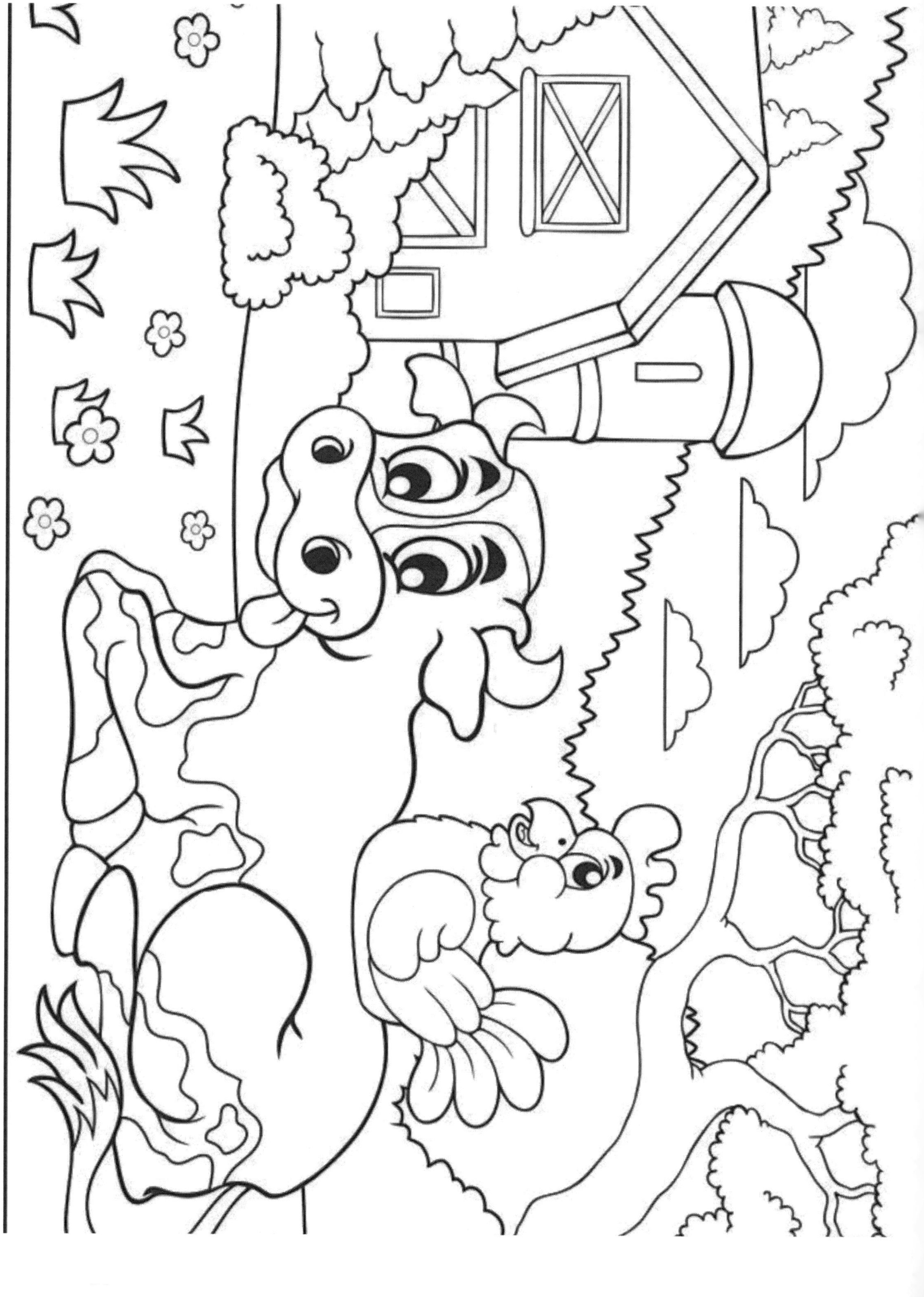

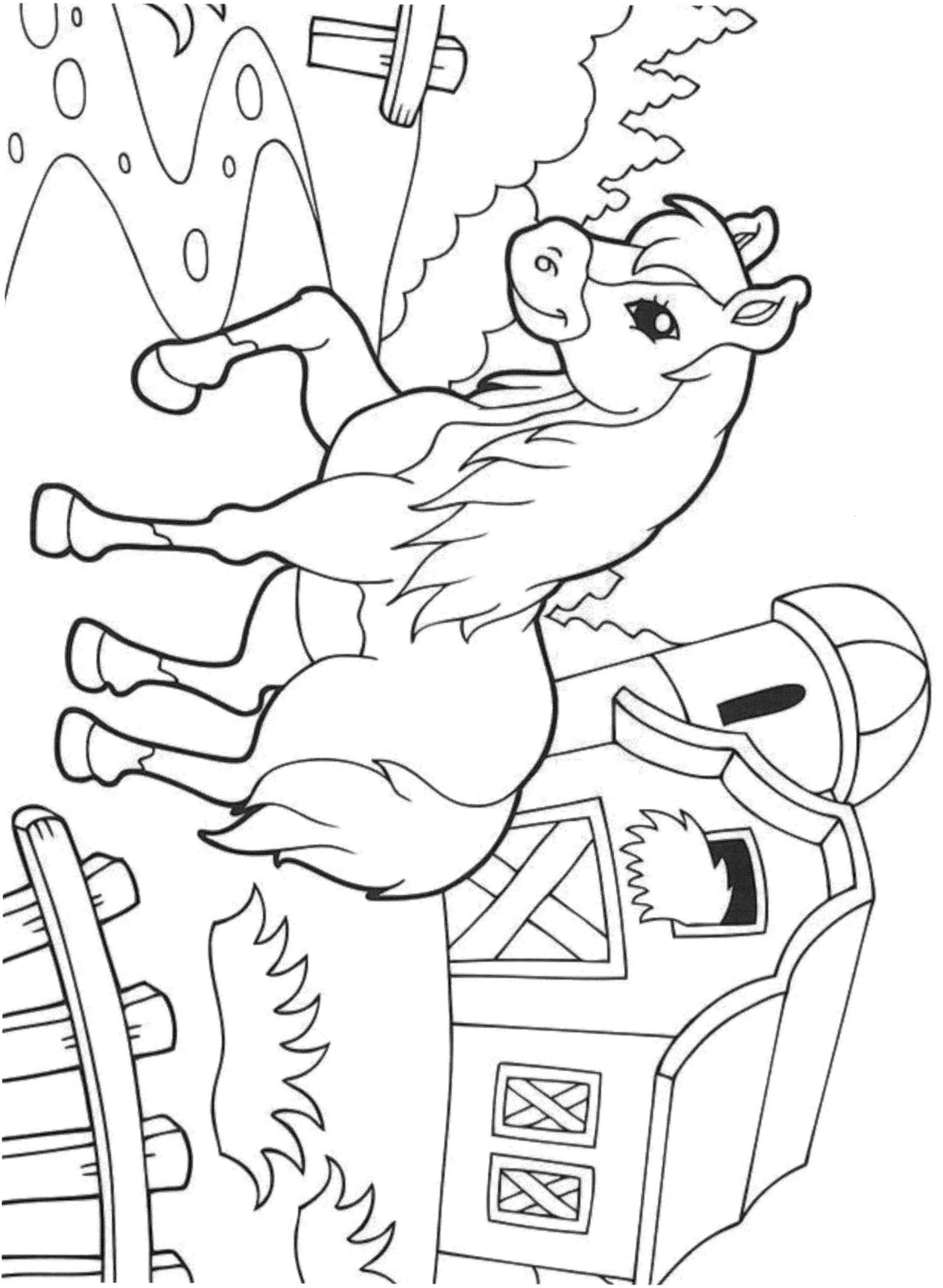

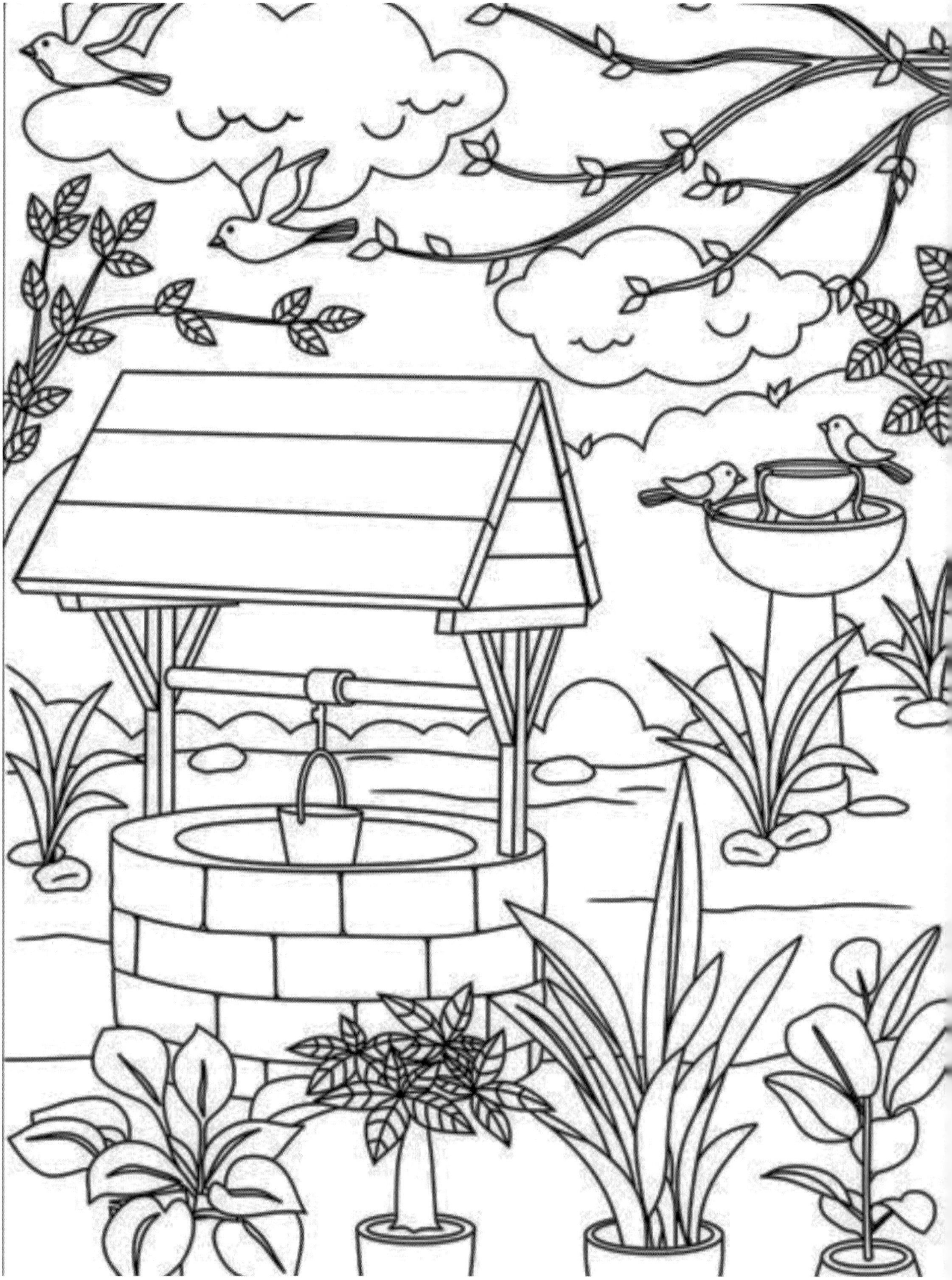

HAPPY
HEN HOUSE
Fresh
Eggs for
Sale

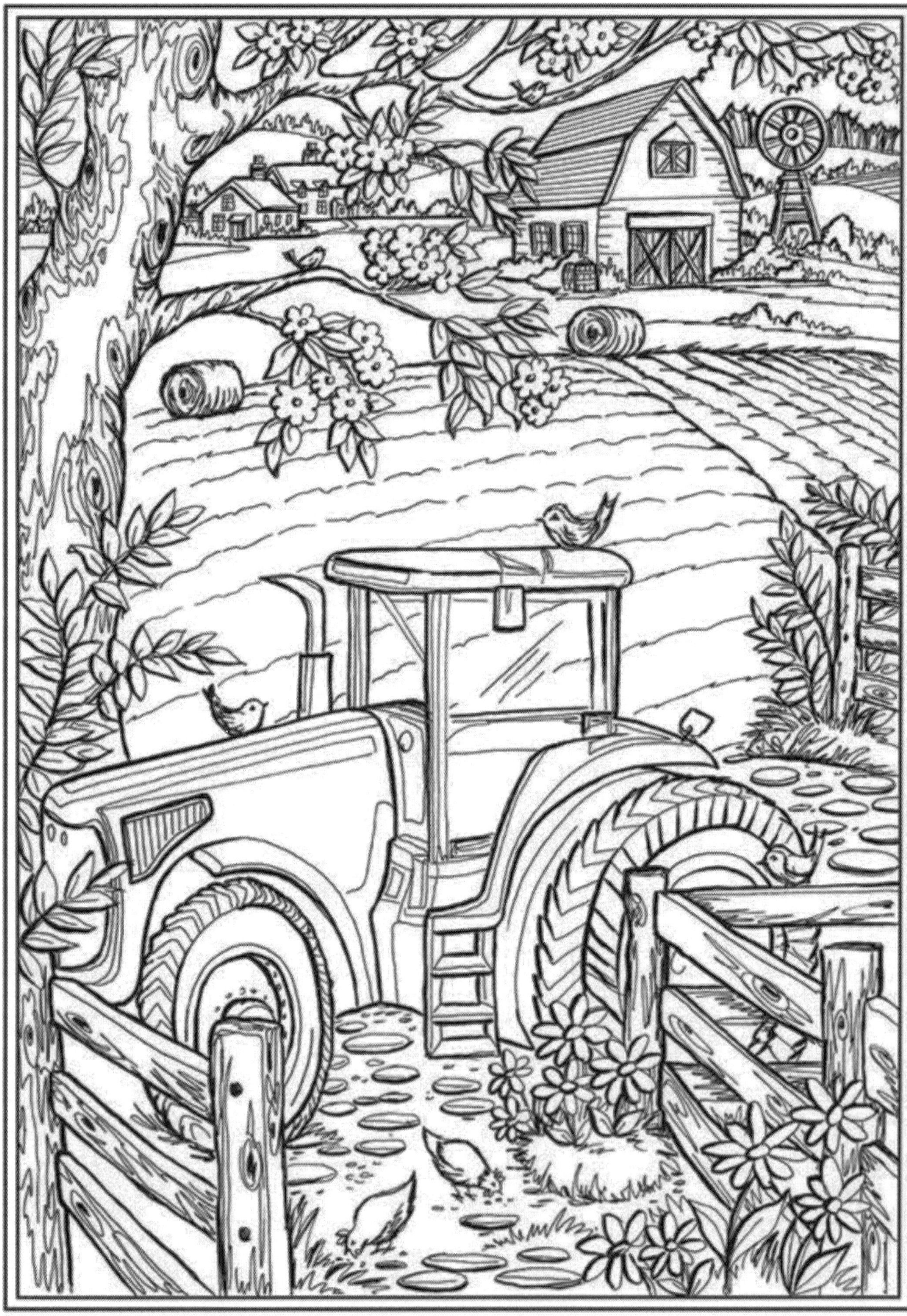

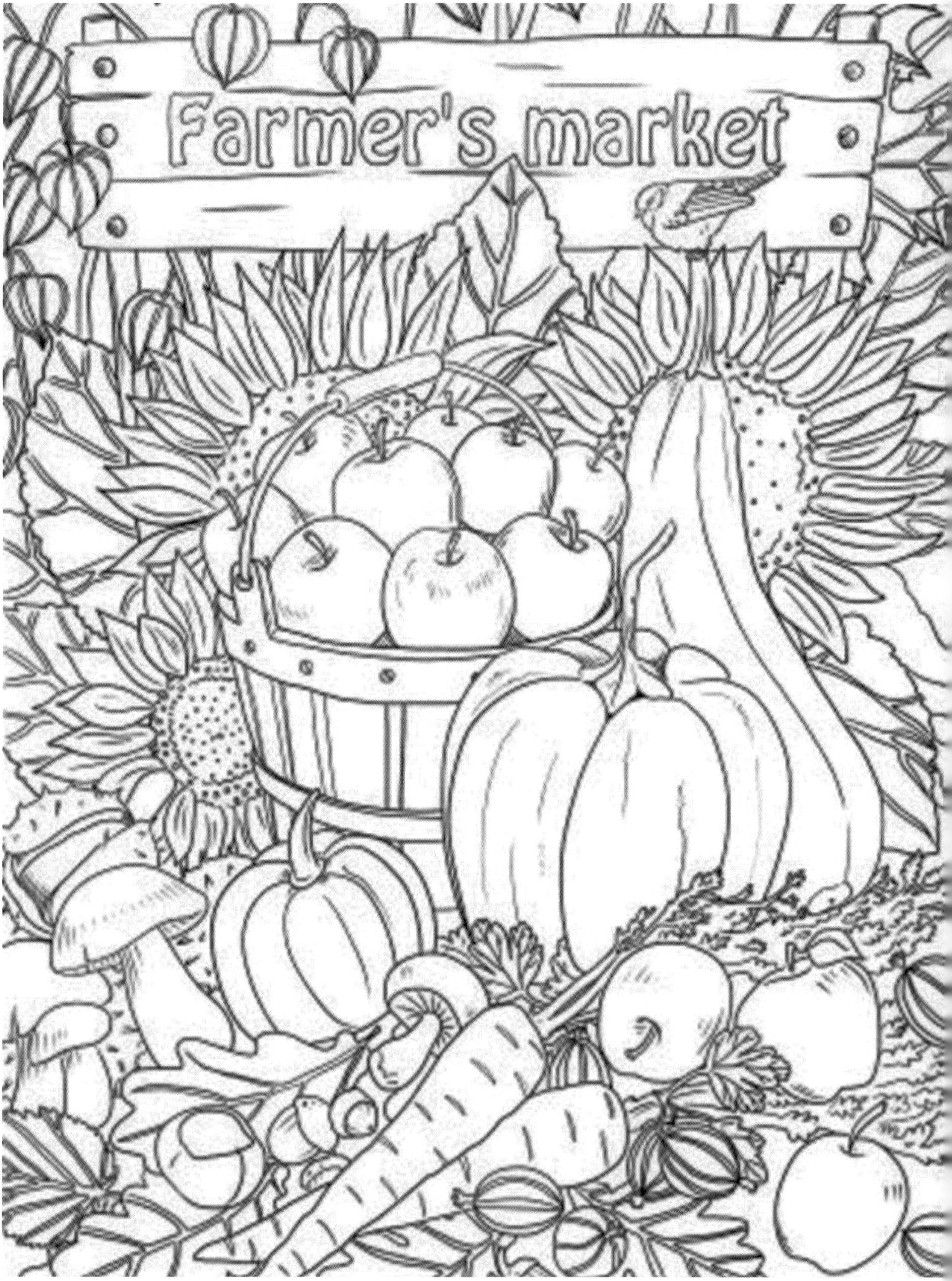
Farmer's market

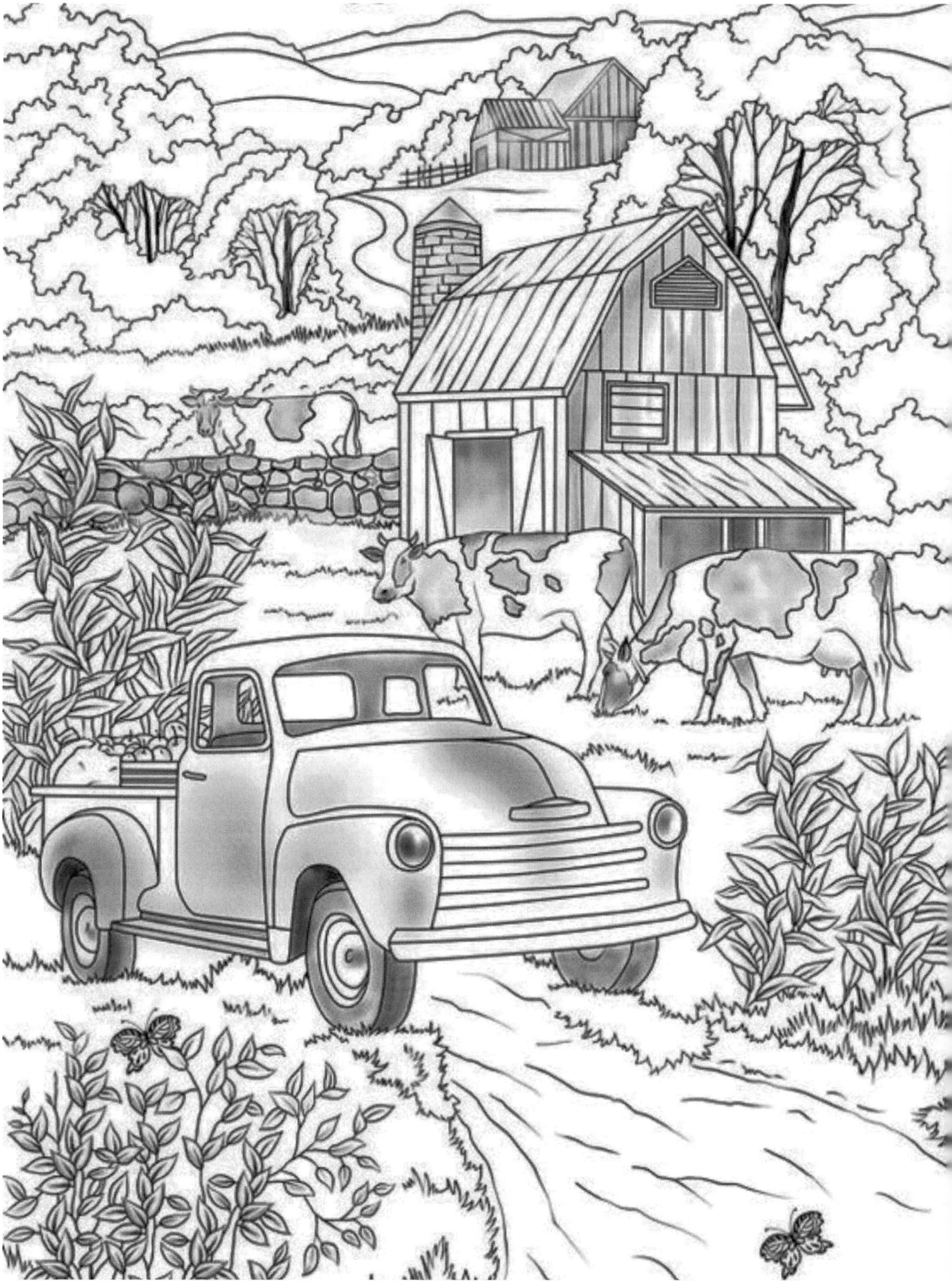

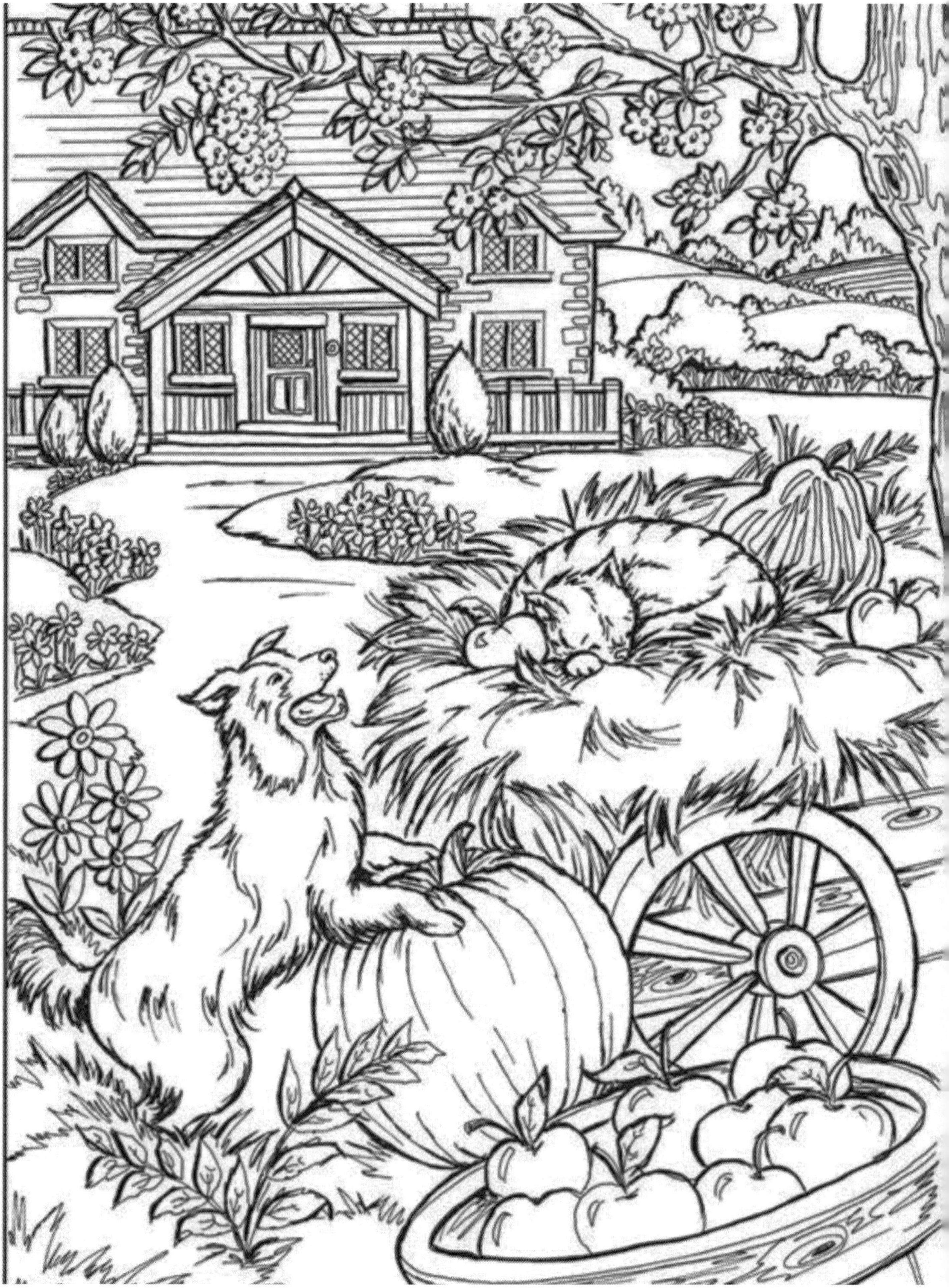

Made in the USA
Monee, IL
23 November 2021

82906449R00035